BARCELONA

CULT RECIPES

STEPHAN MITSCH
PHOTOS BY ARNOLD PÖSCHL

BARCELONA

CULT RECIPES

murdoch books

Sydney | London

CONTENTS

THERE IS NO PARADISE.
GOD LIVES HERE!

Barcelona, this old yet eternally young city, is one of only a few in the world that has successfully reinvented itself. The city underwent major refurbishment for the Olympic Games in 1992, when it was given a new public transport system, a new airport and even completely new suburbs. Since then, it has slowly but surely become a top destination for tourists from all over the world. And they're right: Barcelona is definitely worth a visit, for so much more than sightseeing.

Barcelona, the capital of the Spanish region of Catalonia, has always attracted lots of people. Migrants from poorer areas of Spain, including the regions of Andalusia, Extremadura and Galicia, came as early as the 19th century in search of a better life. They brought not only their customs from their native regions but also their recipes. No need to deprive yourself! This is how Barcelonian cuisine came to incorporate many different influences: gazpacho from Andalusia, paella from Valencia, marmitako from the Basque country and many other dishes. Later, migrants from the Near, Middle and Far East, from Africa and from South and Central America brought even more colour to the culinary potpourri that is this city. Cassava, plantains, sweet potatoes, mung beans, ginger, curry and soy sauce have all become fixtures in Barcelonian cuisine, which is a true *cocina de fusión*.

I've never come across any other city that makes it so easy to spoil yourself with truly amazing food at such reasonable prices. The Mediterranean Sea is right at the city's doorstep, and the surrounding regions are veritable treasure troves of culinary delights. The almost limitless selection of fish and seafood in *La boquería*, Barcelona's best-known market, invites you to explore the city's rich food culture. El Prat de Llobregat, the delta of the Llobregat river south-west of Barcelona, is the city's kitchen garden, where delicious *calçots* (spring onions/scallions) and cabbages are grown in winter and fantastic artichokes and broad beans in spring. Farmers cultivate a huge variety of vegetables here throughout the year, including chickpeas, tomatoes, eggplant (aubergine) and various types of fruit. Catalans are obsessive about mushrooms and cook with vast amounts of them in autumn. This is when red pine mushrooms, chanterelles and Caesar's mushrooms feature prominently on the menus of local restaurants. Traditional Spanish cuisine also uses a lot of rice, not only in the famous paella, and this is also true for Barcelona. Luckily there is a huge rice-growing region a little further south of the city, near Tortosa in the Ebro delta.

Spaniards also love pasta. Filled, large pasta tubes called *canelones* are a traditional Christmas dish, and *escudella i carn d'olla*, the region's famous meat and pasta stew, is a must on major holidays. *Fideos*, a type of thin, short noodles, are very important, too; these are usually cooked together with seafood, mushrooms, vegetables or poultry in the same stock.

Poultry is, of course, very important in traditional Catalan cooking. Chickens, ducks, quail, delectable pheasants and *perdices*, which are quite similar to partridges, are cooked throughout the year according to a seemingly endless variety of recipes. Naturally, meat also plays a major role in Spanish cuisine: there is rabbit, lamb and beef (excellent beef is produced in the neighbouring region around Girona) and, above all, pork. Venison makes its way into Catalan pots and pans in autumn, and 'poor man's meat', that is, snails, also deserve a mention.

One of the outstanding features of Catalan cuisine is dishes that fuse ingredients sourced from the sea and the land (*mar i muntanya*), in combinations that often seem almost outlandish to non-locals. There is bean soup with mussels, rabbit with prawns (shrimp) or chicken with fish and seafood, to name just a few.

Now a few words on dining culture: Spaniards have very frugal breakfasts, often consisting of no more than a cup of coffee at home. On their way to work they might then have a *bocadillo*, that is, a small roll, or a *cruasán*. Simply try to pronounce this – and yes, it is indeed a croissant! If people get hungry before lunch, they can always snack on a few tapas in the late morning, as Spaniards only have lunch from about 2 pm. In the late afternoon, they might then have a few more tapas with a *vermut* or a *caña*, that is, a draught beer. People usually do not come home from work until late, so dinner is also a late affair. Restaurants open at about 8.30 pm at the earliest, and dinner is generally quite rich, especially on weekends. The culinary highlights described on the following page are well worth your attention during a stroll through Barcelona – everything else you'll find in your travel guide!

In the old quarter of El Born/La Ribera you'll find some palaces that are well worth a visit, but most importantly this quarter is home to the Mercat de Santa Caterina, which was fully refurbished a few years ago and fitted with a colourful new roof. Here, you'll find a number of interesting bars and restaurants, for example the 'Cuines Santa Caterina' inside the market. The Gothic quarter of El Raval is right next to Las Ramblas in the city centre. This is where Barcelona's high society moved to between the 17th and 19th centuries in an attempt to escape the dark and narrow lanes of the 'old' part of the city, and this is where you'll find, above all, the world-famous *La boquería* or Mercat de Sant Josep. Sadly, the market has been losing some of its authentic appeal due to a steady stream of tourists, and these days many stalls sell fancy colourful fruit cocktails rather than fruit and vegetables. However, if you are lucky enough to find a seat in the 'El Quim de la Boquería' or in the 'Pinotxo', you'll be spoiled with authentic dishes. Even Raval still has some good restaurants, for example the stunningly beautiful 'Fonda España' in the Hotel España or the 'Ca l'Isidre', a true bastion of traditional Catalan cuisine. The old, recently re-opened brewery Moritz in the quarter of Sant Antoni serves beer on tap. The quarter of Eixample ('extension'), which was built as recently as the turn of the 20th century, also has a wealth of interesting restaurants, as do the quarters of Gràcia, Sant Gervasi and Sarrià. I'll only mention three examples: 'Tragaluz', 'Osmosis' and 'Etapes', but there are plenty more, and shops in the little side streets sell anything and everything to do with food and cooking. If you love fish and seafood, you may want to head for the restaurants of Barceloneta, which was the fishermen's quarter a long time ago. Newer quarters such as Poblenou, which was built for the Olympic Games, or 22@, also have a great restaurant culture. The latter is home to the ESHOB – the Barcelona School of Culinary Arts and Gastronomy.

The Catalan master chef Ferran Adrià revolutionised the international culinary world with his ground-breaking creations, and his style of molecular cooking has also had a clear influence on Barcelonian cuisine. His cuisine, which is everything but traditional and combines aromas, colours and textures to appeal to all senses, demonstrates that food and eating can be so much more than merely taking in nutrients. Catalan cuisine, which is widely known for fusing traditional and new elements in many wonderful ways, for transforming conventional ingredients with outstanding creativity and for preserving traditional cooking methods, has also opened up to Ferran Adrià's ideas.

All of these influences have created one of the tastiest cuisines in all of Europe. I'll introduce the dishes under their traditional Catalan and Spanish names as well as with an English translation. Some dishes are only known under their Catalan or Spanish names, though.

So, a few words about myself. How did I end up in Barcelona? That's a long story, but I'll make it short. When I was a child, I was 'transplanted' from Frisia in northern Germany to Ethiopia. I later moved back to Germany, to Düsseldorf, then to Schwetzingen and Frankfurt. I first visited Barcelona a long time before anyone in Germany knew much about the fabulous Catalan cuisine, about 25 years ago. At the time, I didn't try much beyond paella, *gambas al ajillo*, *patatas bravas* and deep-fried fish. But about 15 years ago, I settled in Barcelona. I'm almost pathologically curious and I have absorbed as much as possible of the Catalan lifestyle, culture and language, including the unique local cuisine. Today I'm sure that there is no paradise. God lives here!

A stroll through the narrow lanes in Barcelona's old town helps work up an appetite and is a veritable invitation to indulge in the city's culinary delights.

Once upon a time, tapas was nothing more than a slice of ham or cured meat that was placed on top of a wine glass, mainly in southern Spain, to prevent flies from falling into the wine.

The Spanish word *tapa* simply means 'lid'. But then these little morsels evolved in the most creative of ways. Many dishes that we now know as tapas, for example croquettes or Russian salad, originated as inventive and delicious ways of using up leftovers from the day before. Now that tapas have become a trendy gourmet experience, they are always freshly prepared. These days, you'll find an enormous selection of tapas on offer, and there are tapas bars and even specialised tapas restaurants in Barcelona and elsewhere.

TAPAS

CROQUETES

CROQUETAS | CROQUETTES

Spanish croquettes are very different from what are commonly known as croquettes elsewhere. The first written record of Iberian croquettes goes back to the French author Alexandre Dumas, who enjoyed them during his travels in Spain. Spanish croquettes are based on a relatively firm béchamel sauce that is combined with other ingredients. There are innumerable varieties, but the general preparation always follows the same rules.

1. The béchamel sauce base must be quite firm.

2. The croquettes should all be about the same size, but the shape is irrelevant. The dough should be cold, straight out of a refrigerator, and the croquettes are best shaped using an ice cream scoop.

3. The crumbing step is particularly important: whisk the egg well. For best results, always use freshly crumbed stale bread.

4. Use a small rather than a large pan for deep-frying to ensure that the croquettes are fully immersed in hot oil and cannot break or burst open. Oil for deep-frying has the right temperature if tiny bubbles rise when you drop a trial croquette into the oil. Never try to deep-fry too many croquettes at once!

5. Uncooked croquettes can be frozen and cooked fresh at a later time. Make sure you defrost them fully before deep-frying: there's nothing worse than croquettes that look beautifully golden on the outside but are still frozen and raw inside.

CROQUETES AMB CHORIZO

CROQUETAS CON CHORIZO | CROQUETTES WITH CHORIZO

Here are three traditional variations of plain croquettes.

Makes 40 small croquettes | **Preparation:** 45 minutes
Chilling time: 12 hours, best overnight | **Deep-frying time:** 25–30 minutes

For the croquettes
200 g (7 oz) chorizo

For the béchamel base
100 g (3½ oz) butter
100 g (3½ oz) plain
   (all-purpose) flour
1 litre (35 fl oz) full-cream
   milk
Freshly ground nutmeg

For the coating
2–3 eggs
Breadcrumbs

Also
Plenty of olive oil for
   deep-frying

PREPARE THE DOUGH

Remove the skin from the chorizo and chop the sausage meat finely.
Heat a dry frying pan over medium heat. Fry the chopped chorizo
for a few minutes, stirring. Remove from the pan and drain on
paper towel.

Melt the butter in a large saucepan over medium heat. Add and
sweat the flour, stirring. Be careful not to let it burn. Gradually add
the milk, whisking continuously to prevent lumps from forming.
Season with salt, freshly ground black pepper and nutmeg. Continue
to simmer for another 15 minutes to thicken.

Add the flavouring ingredients, in this case the chorizo, and
simmer for another 5 minutes. Transfer the mixture to a bowl.
Cover with plastic wrap and refrigerate for several hours, ideally
overnight, to allow the mixture to firm up.

SHAPE THE CROQUETTES

Whisk the eggs in a shallow bowl. Transfer the breadcrumbs to a
deep plate. Use an ice cream scoop to divide the béchamel mixture
into balls of equal size. Shape round or oval croquettes. Dip and turn
the croquettes first in the egg, then in the breadcrumbs. Deep-fry in
the hot oil, then drain on paper towel.

VARIATIONS

Croquettes are the perfect base for many different flavourings and
ingredients, including fish (tuna or bacalao/salt cod), seafood,
cheese, vegetables and more. Avoid adding too many ingredients
to any particular type of croquettes, or they may fall apart.

CROQUETES AMB CEPS

CROQUETAS DE SETAS
CROQUETTES WITH MUSHROOMS

Butter for sautéing
1–2 onions, finely chopped
200 g (7 oz) porcini or mixed mushrooms,
finely diced
100 ml (3½ fl oz) robust white wine
1 tablespoon curly parsley, chopped

Melt the butter in a frying pan over medium heat. Add the onions and sauté until golden brown. Add the mushrooms, increase the heat to high and fry. Season the mixture with salt and freshly ground black pepper and deglaze with the white wine. Simmer to reduce.

Remove the mushroom mixture from the pan and drain in a sieve or on paper towel. Mix in the parsley and continue as in the recipe on page 16.

CROQUETES DE POLLO

CROQUETAS DE POLLO
CROQUETTES WITH CHICKEN

Butter for sautéing
2 onions, finely chopped
250 g (9 oz) skinless chicken breast fillet,
finely diced

Melt the butter in a frying pan over medium heat. Add the onions and sauté until golden brown. Add the chicken and sauté for a few minutes, stirring occasionally, then season to taste with salt and freshly ground white pepper.

Remove the chicken mixture from the pan and drain in a sieve or on paper towel. Continue as in the recipe on page 16.

CROQUETES CASOLANES DE ESPINACS

In another version, the béchamel sauce is made using the flavouring ingredient.

Makes 40 small croquettes | **Preparation:** 45 minutes
Chilling time: 12 hours, best overnight | **Deep-frying time:** 25–30 minutes

For the croquettes
200 g (7 oz) frozen
  English spinach
1 pinch salt
80 g (2¾ oz) butter
2 tablespoons plain
  (all-purpose) flour
400 ml (14 fl oz) milk
50 g (1¾ oz) blue-vein
  cheese, crumbled

For the coating
2–3 eggs
Breadcrumbs

Also
Plenty of olive oil for
  deep-frying

Cook the spinach in a little salted water for 5 minutes. Strain through a sieve, drain well and squeeze out the excess water. Melt the butter in a frying pan over medium heat. Add the spinach and sauté briefly. Stir in the flour. Gradually add the milk, stirring constantly until the mixture thickens to a creamy, green béchamel sauce. Take the pan off the heat and fold the crumbled cheese into the hot sauce until it has melted. Refrigerate for 12 hours. Shape into croquettes, crumb and deep-fry (see page 16).

CROQUETES AMB CECINA

CROQUETAS CON CECINA ┊ CROQUETTES WITH CECINA AND LEEKS

Butter for sautéing
1 small leek, finely sliced
150 g (5½ oz) cecina (air-dried beef), finely chopped

Melt the butter in a frying pan over medium heat. Add the leek and sauté until golden brown. Add the cecina. Continue to sauté for a few minutes, stirring occasionally, then season to taste with salt and freshly ground black pepper. Remove the beef mixture from the pan and drain in a sieve or on paper towel. Continue as in the recipe on page 16.

PAN AMB TOMAQUET

PAN CON TOMATE | BREAD WITH TOMATO

This is one of the classics of Catalan cuisine that everyone knows. Barcelonian restaurants often serve this simple dish automatically as a starter. As with so many other dishes of Catalan and Spanish cuisine, it originated as typical peasant food. Stale slices of white bread were not thrown away, but rather rubbed with half a tomacó, *an ancient variety of tomato with a hard skin that keeps the fruit inside fresh for months. Sometimes the bread was also rubbed with a garlic clove. It was then drizzled with olive oil and salt before serving. Traditionally,* pan amb tomaquet *was prepared with a slice of toasted or roasted* pan de pagès, *a type of rustic white bread.*

Preparation: 10 minutes

Garlic cloves
Slices of rustic white bread, best toasted on a hot barbecue
Ripe tomatoes, halved
High-quality cold-pressed olive oil
Coarse salt

If you like, halve a garlic clove and rub the toasted bread with the garlic. Then rub each slice of bread with the fruit of half a tomato. Discard the tomato skin – it isn't used in this recipe. Drizzle the bread generously with olive oil and sprinkle with a pinch of coarse salt – done.

Pan amb tomaquet makes an incredibly delicious and easy starter or snack.

MANDONGUILLES AMB PÉSOLS

ALBÓNDIGAS CON GUISANTES | MEATBALLS WITH PEAS

*Who doesn't know and love delicious meatballs, served in a rich sauce? The irresistible
smell of these little delicacies wafts through many tapas bars in Barcelona.*

Serves 4 | **Preparation:** 15 minutes | **Cooking and frying time:** 1 hour 5 minutes

For the sauce

4 tablespoons olive oil
1 small red capsicum
   (pepper), finely diced
1 small green capsicum
   (pepper), finely diced
1 carrot, finely diced
2 tomatoes, finely diced
1 large onion, finely diced
1 small garlic clove, minced
200 ml (7 fl oz) vegetable
   stock
240 g (8½ oz) can peas

For the meatballs

1 egg
2 slices stale white
   bread, diced
½ glass white wine
1 kg (2 lb 4 oz) mixed
   minced (ground) meat
2 tablespoons plain
   (all-purpose) flour

PREPARE THE SAUCE

Heat 1 tablespoon olive oil in a saucepan over medium heat.
Add the capsicums, carrot, tomatoes, onion and garlic and sauté
for 6–8 minutes. Season with salt and freshly ground black pepper.
Blend thoroughly with a stick blender and return to the saucepan.
Add the vegetable stock and heat everything through.

PREPARE AND FRY THE MEATBALLS

Meanwhile, combine the egg, bread, white wine and a little salt
in a bowl. Add the minced meat and knead everything to form a
dough. Transfer the flour to a shallow plate. Shape the meat mixture
into balls of about 4 cm (1½ inches) diameter. Roll in the flour to
prevent them from falling apart during frying.

Heat the remaining olive oil in a deep frying pan over medium
heat and fry the meatballs until golden brown. Transfer the meatballs
to the sauce. Increase the heat slightly and cook the meatballs until
done, about 30 minutes. Add the peas to the sauce and simmer for
another 10 minutes. Serve hot in individual ceramic bowls.

VARIATION:

To make mandonguilles a la jardinera, only add half of the peas
to the blended sauce before heating. Substitute the other half with
diced carrot and add 150 g (5½ oz) small button mushrooms.

SEITONS EN VINAGRE

BOQUERONES EN VINAGRE | PICKLED ANCHOVIES

Seitons or boquerones en vinagre are among the stand-out tapas in Barcelonian bars. The origins of this recipe, which was imported by migrant workers, can be traced back to Andalusia. Pickled in vinegar, oil, garlic and parsley and served on a slice of baguette rubbed with half a tomato, these anchovies are simply exquisite. They have been known to entice even people averse to fish, especially raw fish!

Serves 4 | **Preparation:** 45 minutes | **Marinating time:** at least 4 hours

500 g (1 lb 2 oz) fresh anchovies (ideally gutted by a fishmonger)
400 ml (14 fl oz) wine vinegar
1 teaspoon salt
1 garlic clove, thinly sliced
1 teaspoon sweet paprika
Cold-pressed olive oil
Flat-leaf (Italian) parsley, thinly sliced

PREPARE THE ANCHOVIES

Carefully wash the fresh anchovies and snap off the heads towards the spines. Use your thumb to slice open the fish from this opening towards the tail and remove the guts. Rinse the remaining fillets and remove the central bone and all attached bones, starting from the tail. It is easier, though, to have your fishmonger prepare the fish. Transfer the prepared anchovy fillets to a bowl with iced water and leave for about 20 minutes to remove any impurities.

MARINATE THE ANCHOVIES

Combine the wine vinegar, salt and garlic well in a ceramic or plastic bowl. Add the anchovies, refrigerate and marinate for at least 4 hours, but no more than 24 hours – if marinating for an extended period, dilute the marinade with a little more vinegar. The fish should be completely covered with the marinade.

PUT THE DISH TOGETHER

To serve, remove the anchovies from the marinade, but do not drain them. Reserve the marinade. Arrange the anchovies on a plate and dust with a little paprika to taste. Drizzle with olive oil and sprinkle with parsley and the sliced garlic from the marinade. As an alternative, serve on a slice of bread rubbed with half a tomato.

Covered with marinade or oil, these anchovies will keep for 2–3 days in the refrigerator.

GAMBAS AL AJILLO

GAMBAS AL AJILLO | PRAWNS IN GARLIC SAUCE

Gambas al ajillo *are not only among the best-known tapas,*
they are also easy to prepare and incredibly delicious.

Serves 4 | **Preparation:** 10 minutes | **Cooking time:** 15 minutes

3 garlic cloves, thinly sliced
2 red chillies, seeded and
  thinly sliced
250 ml (9 fl oz) olive oil
100 g (3½ oz) prawns
  (shrimp), peeled and
  deveined with tails intact

Gently fry the sliced garlic and chillies in a little of the olive oil in a deep frying pan or casserole dish. Add the prawns as soon as the garlic starts to colour and briefly fry everything together. Add the remaining olive oil, heat everything over medium heat and season with a little salt. Serve immediately with white bread, either straight from the pan or in four warmed ceramic bowls.

ENSALADILLA RUSA

ENSALADILLA RUSA | RUSSIAN SALAD

Ensaladilla rusa is yet another popular tapa in bars all over Barcelona. It was originally a way of using up leftovers.

Serves 4 | **Preparation:** 10 minutes | **Chilling time:** 2–3 hours

200 g (7 oz) waxy potatoes,
   boiled and diced
300 g (10½ oz) green beans,
   cooked and cut into
   short lengths
300 g (10½ oz) peas,
   cooked (alternatively
   use canned peas)
300 g (10½ oz) carrots,
   cooked and finely diced
1 tomato, peeled, seeded
   and finely diced
Home-made mayonnaise
   (see recipe on page 260)

Toss all of the vegetables in a bowl to combine. Fold in the mayonnaise. Season with salt and freshly ground white pepper. Refrigerate the salad for 2–3 hours before serving.

PATATES BRAVES

PATATAS BRAVAS | PATATAS BRAVAS

Patatas bravas are eaten all over Spain. These 'wild potatoes' are served with salsa brava, a flavourful sauce that should never see ketchup, even though these days it is (unfortunately) often replaced by a milder mixture of ketchup and tomatoes. Actually mayonnaise isn't a traditional ingredient either, but I just love it. The best-tasting and most popular bravas in all of Barcelona are served at 'Casa Tomás' in Sarrià, where they are prepared with all i oli instead of mayonnaise.

Serves 4 | **Preparation:** 30 minutes | **Cooking and frying time:** 30 minutes

For the salsa brava
2 tablespoons olive oil
1 onion, finely diced
1 tablespoon sweet paprika
1 tablespoon hot paprika
2–3 tablespoons plain
  (all-purpose) flour
100 g (3½ oz) canned
  tomato purée
400 ml (14 fl oz) chicken
  stock

For the potatoes
Olive oil for deep-frying
2 large potatoes, cut into
  2.5 cm (1 inch) thick strips

Plus
Home-made mayonnaise
  (see recipe on page 260)

PREPARE THE SALSA BRAVA
Warm the olive oil in a frying pan over medium heat. Add the onion and sweat until translucent. Stir in the paprika carefully, as paprika burns easily and then turns bitter. Stir in the flour, then add the puréed tomatoes and chicken stock. Simmer to reduce a little. Season with salt. Salsa brava will keep for a good week in the refrigerator.

FRY AND PLATE THE POTATOES
Heat the olive oil in a deep frying pan or casserole dish over very high heat. Add the potatoes and fry for 2 minutes. Reduce the temperature and continue to cook for another 5–6 minutes. Increase the temperature again for the final 2 minutes until the potatoes turn golden brown.

Drain the potatoes on paper towel and season with salt. Serve with a dollop of mayonnaise and a generous drizzle of salsa brava.

BOMBETAS DE PATATES FARCIDES

BOMBAS DE PATATAS RELLENAS | STUFFED POTATO BALLS

This delectably simple dish is a staple in many tapas bars. The potato balls can be served warm or cold. They are especially popular in the old town of Barcelona and in Barceloneta.

Makes 12–14 potato balls | **Preparation:** 25 minutes | **Cooking and frying time:** 30 minutes

400 g (14 oz) floury potatoes
1 onion
1 small garlic clove
200 g (7 oz) mixed minced (ground) meat
100 g (3½ oz) canned tomato purée
1 teaspoon Tabasco sauce
Freshly ground nutmeg
Olive oil for frying and for the potato dough
3–4 tablespoons plain (all-purpose) flour
3–4 tablespoons breadcrumbs
2 eggs
Home-made mayonnaise (see recipe on page 260)
Salsa brava (see recipe on page 30)

PREPARE THE MINCED MEAT MIXTURE

Scrub the potatoes and boil until tender with the skins on. Meanwhile, peel and mince the onion and garlic. Heat a frying pan over medium heat. Add the onion, garlic and minced meat and fry briefly. Once the meat has browned all over, add the tomato purée and Tabasco and season with salt. Continue to cook for another 10 minutes, stirring constantly, until all of the liquid has evaporated.

MAKE AND COOK THE POTATO BALLS

Peel the cooked potatoes once they are cool enough to handle. Transfer to a bowl and mash thoroughly with a fork. Season well with salt, freshly ground black pepper, nutmeg and 1–2 tablespoons olive oil. This should make a soft dough that is still easy to shape.

Shape the potato dough into 12–14 balls. Flatten the balls and place a small amount of the minced meat mixture in the centre. Carefully shape into balls again around the filling. Transfer the flour and breadcrumbs to separate shallow bowls. Whisk the eggs in a third bowl. Turn the balls in the flour, then dip them into the whisked eggs and roll them in the breadcrumbs.

Deep-fry the balls in plenty of olive oil over high heat until golden brown. Drain on paper towel. Serve with home-made mayonnaise and salsa brava.

PIMIENTOS DE PADRÓN

PIMIENTOS DE PADRÓN | DEEP-FRIED PADRÓN CHILLIES

Pimientos de padrón *originally come from the region around the city of Padrón. Until about 20 years ago, they were mainly found in Galician tapas bars in Barcelona, but these days they are a fixture on the menu of virtually any tapas bar in the city. Part of the original fun was that padrón chillies used to be rather unpredictable. About one in six or eight chillies on the plate would be hot, and about one in ten or twelve fiercely so – but there was no way of telling from just looking. Any hot surprises were taken in good spirits, though, and with a lot of laughter. These days,* pimientos de padrón *are available from many well-stocked greengrocers and supermarkets.*

Serves 4 | **Preparation:** 15 minutes | **Deep-frying time:** 5 minutes

250 g (9 oz) padrón chillies
Olive oil for deep-frying
Fleur de sel

Wash the chillies and dry well. Heat the olive oil in a saucepan or deep-fryer and fry the chillies until the skins begin to blister all over and develop a few dark brown spots. Briefly drain on paper towel. Transfer to a plate, sprinkle with coarse fleur de sel salt and serve immediately.

WHO

eat

ways THE

PEOPLE

OUS ESTRELLATS

HUEVOS ESTRELLADOS | FRIED EGGS AND POTATOES

*Eggs and potatoes always make an excellent combination for which there seems to exist
an endless variety of recipes. The 'Vermutería Lou' won a prize for this recipe in the
2014 Barcelona tapas competition. Try it and you'll know why!*

Serves 4 | **Preparation:** 10 minutes | **Cooking time:** 15 minutes

Plenty of olive oil
4 potatoes, cut into 2.5 cm
   (1 inch) dice or into chips
4 very fresh eggs
Iberian ham, cut into
   thin strips

FRY THE POTATOTES

Heat plenty of olive oil in a deep frying pan or casserole dish over
very high heat. Add the potatoes and fry for 2 minutes over high
heat. Reduce the temperature and cook the potatoes for another
5–6 minutes. Increase the temperature again and cook for another
2 minutes until the potatoes are golden brown. Drain the potatoes
on paper towel and season with salt.

FRY THE EGGS

Heat plenty of olive oil in another frying pan. Crack the eggs and
slide into the pan. Fry, continually basting with hot olive oil. The
idea is to have the egg whites set fully while keeping the egg yolks
beautifully runny.

Divide the potatoes among four ceramic bowls. Slide 1 egg on
top of each. Season the eggs with a little salt and top with strips of
ham. Serve immediately. Allow the hot egg yolks to burst over the
potatoes, if preferred.

BRANDADA DE BACALAO

BRANDADA DE BACALAO | PURÉED BACALAO

There are a number of different versions of brandada de bacalao, *all of which make popular starters across the region extending from the Basque country to Catalonia and Catalan-speaking France. This easy recipe is always a winner.*

Serves 4 | **Preparation:** 20 minutes | **Cooking time:** 25 minutes

400 g (14 oz) bacalao (salt cod), desalted, without skin or bones, diced
250 g (9 oz) floury potatoes
300 ml (10½ fl oz) olive oil
1 garlic clove, thinly sliced
100 ml (3½ fl oz) cream, gently warmed

COOK THE BACALAO

Bring plenty of water to the boil in a pot. Add the bacalao and simmer for 2 minutes, making sure that it is well covered with water. Remove the bacalao and drain well. Reserve a little of the cooking water.

BOIL THE POTATOES

Peel the potatoes and boil them in a pan of salted water. Meanwhile, heat the olive oil in a saucepan over medium heat. Gently fry the garlic slices until golden brown, being careful not to burn them, as they then turn bitter. Remove from the oil and set aside.

Remove the saucepan from the heat and add the bacalao to the hot oil. The fish will cook perfectly in the heat retained in the oil.

Drain the potatoes. Combine with the cream and mash thoroughly. If necessary or preferred, add a little of the reserved cooking liquid. Season to taste with salt and freshly ground white pepper.

PUT TOGETHER THE BRANDADA

Transfer the mashed potatoes, bacalao and garlic to a blender. Blend well. Add the olive oil to the running blender in a steady stream until the cream firms up a little. Season to taste with salt and white pepper.

Spread thickly on slices of toasted baguette and garnish with parsley, pickled capsicums or caviar. Alternatively, serve with sliced potatoes and paprika.

PIMIENTOS DEL PIQUILLO FARCITS

PIMIENTOS DEL PIQUILLO RELLENOS | STUFFED PIQUILLO PEPPERS

In Barcelona, there is no tapas bar worth its salt that does not feature this little delicacy on its menu. Pimientos del piquillo are made of red piquillo peppers, which are about 7–10 cm (2¾–4 inches) long and whose shape is reminiscent of liberty caps. Raw piquillos are too bitter for eating, so they are first roasted over an open fire and then peeled and seeded by hand. This gives them a mild, smoky aroma and a pleasantly spicy, sweet and sour flavour. Piquillos are only available in jars or cans. They can be stuffed with a variety of fillings and used for any number of wonderful tapas and starters.

Serves 2 | **Preparation:** 1½ hours | **Cooking time:** 15 minutes

For the pimientos

100 ml (3½ fl oz) olive oil, plus extra for sautéing and frying
300 g (10½ oz) bacalao (salt cod), desalted, without skin or bones, cut into two pieces
150 ml (5 fl oz) cream
2–3 garlic cloves, peeled
1 dried chilli
2 tablespoons flat-leaf (Italian) parsley, finely chopped
8 red piquillo peppers

For the sauce

100 ml (3½ fl oz) olive oil
2 garlic cloves, thinly sliced
2 red piquillo peppers
300 ml (10½ fl oz) cream

COOK THE BACALAO

Heat 100 ml (3½ fl oz) olive oil in a frying pan over low heat, making sure the temperature never exceeds 90°C (195°F). Add the bacalao to the oil. (Alternatively, remove the pan from the heat and gently cook the bacalao in the residual heat, gently shaking the pan.) The fish will release a milky liquid, which will emulsify with the oil. Carefully turn the fish after 10 minutes, then continue cooking for another 5 minutes. Remove the fish from the oil and set aside to cool.

Meanwhile, heat the cream in a saucepan over low heat and reduce carefully. Heat a little olive oil in another pan over very low heat. Add the garlic and chilli and sauté until golden to flavour the oil. Discard the garlic and chilli.

PREPARE THE FILLING

Carefully pull the bacalao into pieces with a fork, removing and discarding the skin. Transfer to a bowl and combine with the chopped parsley. Slowly add the flavoured oil and the reduced cream and whisk everything to combine to a thick paste. Season with salt and freshly ground white pepper. Use a piping bag or small spoon to fill the piquillo peppers about three-quarters full with the bacalao mixture. Set aside.

Preheat the oven to 160°C (320°F).

PREPARE THE SAUCE

For the sauce, heat the olive oil in a saucepan over medium heat.
Add the garlic and gently fry until golden brown. Remove from
the oil. Add the piquillo peppers to the hot oil. Add the cream
and simmer for 5 minutes, then season with salt and white pepper.
Blend everything well with a stick blender, then reduce a little more.

Arrange the stuffed peppers in a ceramic bowl, spoon the sauce
on top and place in the hot oven to heat through for a few minutes
before serving.

ESQUEIXADA

ESQUEIXADA | BACALAO AND VEGETABLE SALAD

An esqueixada, *pronounced 'es-cay-shah-da', is a unique type of salad. It is prepared with desalted, raw bacalao and various vegetables. Not only does it take next to no time to prepare, it also makes a very refreshing and healthy snack on a hot summer's day. Like many other simple, classic dishes,* esqueixada *also comes in many different versions, so feel free to experiment with any seasonal vegetables you like.*

Serves 4 | **Preparation:** 15 minutes | **Marinating time:** 30 minutes

300 g (10½ oz) tomatoes
600 g (1 lb 5 oz) bacalao
   (salt cod), desalted,
   without skin or bones
1 green capsicum (pepper)
1 red capsicum (pepper)
2 red onions
200 ml (7 fl oz) olive oil
4 tablespoons vinegar
150 g (5½ oz) black
   olives, diced

Dice the tomatoes finely. Squeeze out the excess water from the bacalao and cut it into bite-sized pieces. Refrigerate the diced tomatoes and fish.

Trim the capsicums and onions and finely dice. Transfer to a bowl, dress with olive oil and vinegar and toss to combine. Season with salt and freshly ground black pepper.

Refrigerate for 30 minutes to allow the flavours to marry, then put the dish together using ring moulds. First add the tomatoes to the moulds, followed by the bacalao. Top with the marinated vegetables and press down gently. Drizzle with the marinade and garnish with the olives. Remove the ring moulds before serving.

XIPS DE CARXOFES

CHIPS DE ALCACHOFAS | ARTICHOKE CHIPS

Barcelona is truly blessed with its location, with the Mediterranean Sea on one side and the Baix-Llobregat, the fertile delta of the Llobregat river, in the city's south-west. Farmers have produced excellent vegetables in this delta for centuries. Particularly good are the local habas *(broad beans) and artichokes, which even have their own denomination of origin (DO). In good years with mild winters, fresh artichokes are available as early as December – and as cheap as potatoes! Artichokes deserve a lot better than being drowned in a vinaigrette. Deep-fried artichokes, for example, are a lot healthier than potato chips and a lot tastier, too. A thoroughly delectable tapa!*

Serves 4 | Preparation: 10 minutes | **Deep-frying time:** 5 minutes

4–8 small Spanish
  artichokes
Olive oil or sunflower oil
  for deep-frying

Clean and trim the artichokes. Remove the fibrous chokes and cut the hearts lengthwise into 3 mm (⅛ inch) slices. Heat the oil in a saucepan and quickly add the sliced artichokes to prevent oxidation. Deep-fry until golden brown. Drain on paper towel, season with a little salt and serve hot.

I always suggest that people wear gloves when working with artichokes. Spotty brown hands aren't a great sight.

CABDELLS AMB CABRALES AL FORN

COGOLLOS CON CABRALES AL HORNO | BAKED LETTUCE HEARTS WITH CABRALES

Cabrales, an intensely flavoured blue-vein cheese, comes from the village of the same name. When still young, it tastes like a mild gorgonzola. As it matures, it develops a fuller flavour, similar to roquefort, and fully mature it becomes quite strong. Witlof (chicory) makes an excellent alternative for preparing this dish.

Serves 4 | Preparation: 15 minutes | **Cooking time:** 5 minutes

4 small cos (romaine)
  lettuce hearts
Cabrales or other blue-vein
  cheese to taste

Preheat the oven grill (broiler) to medium heat.

Remove any tough or unsightly outer leaves from the lettuce hearts. Wash and shake dry the lettuces. Halve or quarter, depending on size, and top with cheese to taste. Cook under the preheated grill for a few minutes and serve immediately.

PA ROSTIT AMB PATE DE TOMAQUET

PAN TOSTADO CON PATÉ DE TOMATE | GRILLED BREAD WITH TOMATO PASTE

Barcelona is a very creative city in every respect, and so it doesn't come as a surprise that cafés and bars also display almost unlimited ingenuity when it comes to tapas. One of these cafés is 'Caelum, delicias y otras tentaciones de Monasterio', and its name says it all: 'heaven, delicacies and other temptations from the monastery'. This is also precisely its mission, as the café offers beverages, sweets, pastries and more, all made in local monasteries, for enjoying on the premises or taking home. Its kitchen is the home of this elegant starter: toasted bread with tomato paste and brie.

Serves 4 | **Preparation:** 15 minutes | **Cooking time:** 5 minutes

4 sun-dried tomatoes
  in oil, drained
1 anchovy fillet in oil
Mushroom powder to taste
100 g (3½ oz) black
  olive paste
200 g (7 oz) brie cheese
1 baguette, sliced diagonally
  into 8 pieces

Slice the tomatoes and anchovy fillet as thinly as possible. Pound both to a paste using a mortar and pestle. Season with mushroom powder to taste. Add the olive paste and mix to combine.

Preheat the oven grill (broiler) to medium heat. Cut the brie into slices to fit the baguette slices. Top each baguette slice with a slice of brie. Spread generously with the tomato and olive paste. Cook under the preheated grill until the cheese starts to melt. Serve immediately.

ANEM DE TAPES…

… is what people say in Barcelona when they want to catch up with friends, have a drink and eat a couple of tapas. What then usually happens is that they move from one bar to the next, and a glass of wine or just one beer with a few tapas quickly turns into a full dinner and a cheerful evening in great company.

One of Barcelona's most beautiful quarters, El Born/La Ribera, is home to quite a few very typical tapas bars. There is 'El Xampanyet' opposite the Picasso museum, a true classic, or the 'Sagardí', which serves Basque tapas on thick slices of white bread. Everyone helps themselves, and at the end the bill is prepared by counting the empty *palillos* (skewers).

PAQUETS DE FABES

PAQUETES DE HABAS | BROAD BEAN PARCELS

Barcelona wouldn't be Barcelona if it wasn't constantly reinventing itself. While this version of habas a la catalana *is admittedly simple, it can still take its pride of place next to fancier tapas. It makes an innovative starter or snack and will definitely surprise your guests.*

Serves 4 | **Preparation:** 10 minutes | **Cooking time:** 40 minutes

Meat stock
350 g (12 oz) small broad
  beans, shelled
9 large slices of jamón
  Canario or shoulder of
  ham, plus extra if very thin
6–8 fresh mint leaves
Olive oil for frying

Heat the meat stock in a saucepan, add the broad beans and cook for 20–30 minutes over medium heat until soft. Drain well. Season with a little salt, if necessary.

Cut one slice of ham into small pieces and coarsely chop a few of the mint leaves. Combine the chopped ham and mint leaves with the cooked beans.

Divide the bean mixture among eight slices of ham. Make small parcels out of the slices by first folding in the sides on top of the beans, and then folding the ends on top. If the ham is sliced very thinly and tears, place the parcel on top of another slice of ham, seam side down, and repeat the process.

Heat a frying pan over medium heat. Add the olive oil and fry the parcels, seam side down, until crisp. Turn and fry the other side until crisp. Garnish with the remaining mint and serve, if desired, on a bed of the cooked beans.

PATATA, TOMAQUET I SEITONS

PATATAS, TOMATE Y BOQUERONES | POTATO STACKS WITH ANCHOVIES AND TOMATOES

Many tapas, including these boquerones, *can be easily turned into delicious starters. The version described in this recipe makes a simple yet perfect summer dish.*

Serves 4 | **Preparation:** 15 minutes

Baby English spinach
  for garnish
4 potatoes, boiled, peeled
  and cut into 1 cm (½ inch)
  slices (the ends are not
  used in this recipe)
8 sun-dried tomatoes in
  oil, drained
8 whole anchovies in
  vinegar (do not substitute
  with salted anchovies)
A little finely diced Iberian
  ham for garnish
Sea salt flakes
Coarsely ground pink pepper
Olive oil
Vinegar

Lay out the baby spinach in overlapping circles on four plates. Arrange the potato slices, sun-dried tomatoes and anchovies on top of the spinach in alternating layers. This should eventually look similar to the picture on the right. Use a toothpick or skewer to hold the stacks together, if necessary.

Sprinkle the spinach and the potato stacks with some diced ham, sea salt flakes and pink pepper.

Prepare a vinaigrette from olive oil, vinegar, pepper and salt and drizzle over the spinach to make a refreshing summer starter.

FLAN DE GAROÏNES

FLAN DE ERIZOS DE MAR | SEA URCHIN FLAN

An encounter with a sea urchin generally makes for holiday memories that most would rather forget. But there's another way! In spring, people along the Costa Brava organise garoïnades or sea urchin dinners, where each family and each town showcases the best recipes. Sea urchins are true delicacies that do not come cheap, and all that is used for cooking is the sea urchin ovaries, that is the gonads or roe, and the liquid inside. Sea urchins taste neither of fish nor of mussels or caviar, but simply and incomparably of the sea.

Serves 4 | **Preparation:** 15 minutes | **Cooking and baking time:** 45 minutes

For the flan
12 fresh sea urchins
500 ml (17 fl oz) cream
2 g (1/16 oz) saffron
2 eggs
3 egg yolks
Oil or butter for the moulds

For the side
Salad leaves
Vinegar
Olive oil

EXTRACT THE SEA URCHIN ROE

Use a cloth or tea towel to grab the sea urchin with your left hand. Hold it so that the flat bottom is pointing upwards.

Use scissors to cut a circle around the mouth. Pull out this disc together with the attached innards and discard.

Strain the liquid inside the sea urchin through a sieve and reserve.

Inside the sea urchin you'll see five pale orange or red tongue-shaped sections. These are its roe. Carefully remove these using a small spoon. Set aside.

PREPARE THE FLAN

Preheat the oven to 180°C (350°F). Combine the cream and saffron in a saucepan and bring to the boil. Transfer the eggs, egg yolks and sea urchin roe to a bowl and blend with a stick blender. Whisk in the warm saffron cream, then season with salt and freshly ground white pepper.

Divide the mixture among four greased ramekins and bake in the preheated oven for 40 minutes or until set. The cooking time will depend on the size and material of the ramekins – keep checking whether the flans are done by inserting a sharp knife. Remove from the oven, leave to cool and serve with some salad leaves drizzled with a simple vinaigrette of vinegar, olive oil, salt and freshly ground black pepper.

BROMERA DE GAROÏNES

ESPUMA DE ERIZOS DE MAR | SEA URCHIN FOAM

Sea urchin foam is probably the most exquisite of all tapas. It is decoratively served inside the sea urchin shells on a bed of salt. Carefully and evenly enlarge the openings of the sea urchins with sharp kitchen scissors to use the shells for serving.

Serves 4 | **Preparation:** 20 minutes

16 fresh sea urchins
2 egg yolks
4 tablespoons pink cava
   or sparkling rosé wine
4 tablespoons cream
Salt to serve

Remove the sea urchin roe as described on page 58. Clean four of the sea urchin shells and set aside.

Whisk the egg yolks and cava in a double boiler until foamy. Continue whisking until the mixture has the consistency of a sabayon.

Beat the sea urchin roe and cream until foamy using an electric mixer. Pour into a saucepan and heat over low heat, then combine with the 'sabayon'.

Pour the warm mixture into the cleaned shells and serve on a bed of salt, with a teaspoon for eating.

CREMA DE GAROÏNAS

CREMA DE ERIZOS DE MAR | SEA URCHIN CREAM SOUP

Sea urchin can be prepared in a surprising variety of ways. Try this as a soup or use the recipe to make a rather extravagant sauce for fish.

Serves 4 | **Preparation:** 20 minutes | **Cooking time:** 15 minutes

8 fresh sea urchins
10 g (¼ oz) butter
1 French shallot, finely diced
150 ml (5 fl oz) dry white wine
650 ml (22½ fl oz) fish stock
(see recipe on page 261)
2 tablespoons crème
fraîche
2 egg yolks

Remove the sea urchin roe as described on page 58, reserving the strained liquid.

Heat a casserole dish over medium heat. Melt the butter, add the diced shallot and sauté briefly. Deglaze with the wine and reduce by half. Add the fish stock and sea urchin liquid and reduce a little.

Whisk the crème fraîche with the egg yolks until smooth, then gradually whisk the mixture into the stock mixture. Do not allow the mixture to return to the boil, otherwise the egg yolk may curdle.

Strain the thickened soup through a sieve and beat with a stick blender until light and airy. Season with salt and freshly ground white pepper to taste. Just before serving, stir in the sea urchin roe.

If you reduce the amount of fish stock to about 250 ml (9 fl oz) and leave the mixture to reduce a little more, you will have a delicate, creamy sauce with an intense aroma of sea urchin. This sauce matches perfectly with poached or steamed sole or turbot. You'll only need to use four sea urchins.

CREMA DE CARXOFES

CREMA DE ALCACHOFAS | ARTICHOKE CREAM SOUP

*Artichokes are a wonderful vegetable. If it pains you to waste
the trimmed petals, this soup is an excellent solution.*

Serves 4 | **Preparation:** 25 minutes | **Cooking time:** 55 minutes

4 artichokes
Juice of ½ lemon
½ garlic clove, crushed
1 pinch salt
2 tablespoons olive oil
25 g (1 oz) butter
2 onions, chopped
400 ml (14 fl oz) chicken
   or vegetable stock
1 pinch cayenne pepper
20 g (¾ oz) plain
   (all-purpose) flour
250 ml (9 fl oz) cream
2 tablespoons flat-leaf
   (Italian) parsley

Cut off and peel the artichoke stems and immediately drop
them into a bowl of water with half of the lemon juice added.
Remove the artichoke petals and peel them down to the hearts.
Also remove the inner petals directly above the artichoke
hearts. Immediately drop the petals into the bowl of acidulated
water to prevent them from oxidising. Remove and discard the
fibrous chokes from the hearts.

Combine 1 litre (35 fl oz) water, the remaining lemon juice,
garlic, salt and olive oil in a large saucepan and bring to the boil.
Add the artichoke hearts and stems. Simmer for about 25 minutes
or until they can be easily pierced with a fork, but still hold their
shape. Remove from the saucepan and set aside. Add the artichoke
petals to the saucepan, bring to the boil and simmer for 25 minutes
over low heat. Remove the petals from the cooking liquid and blend
them to a fine paste using a stick blender. Pass the paste through a
sieve. Strain the cooking liquid through a sieve and reserve 350 ml
(12 fl oz). Slice the artichoke hearts and dice the stems. Set aside.

FINISH THE ARTICHOKE CREAM SOUP

Melt the butter in a saucepan over medium heat. Add the onions
and sauté briefly. Add the stock, artichoke paste and reserved
cooking liquid and season with salt and cayenne pepper. Combine
the flour with a little cream and whisk into the soup to thicken.
Add the remaining cream and briefly bring to the boil, adding the
sliced artichoke hearts and diced stems just before the mixture
comes to the boil. Serve garnished with parsley.

CREMA DE CARXOFES I CURRI

CREMA DE ALCACHOFAS Y CURRY | CURRIED ARTICHOKE CREAM

Artichokes are an incredibly versatile vegetable that can be combined with many different ingredients and spices – in this case with curry.

Serves 4 | **Preparation:** 20 minutes | **Cooking time:** 1 hour 10 minutes

4 artichokes
Juice of 1 lemon
2 tablespoons olive oil
1 onion, finely diced
200 g (7 oz) carrots, diced
2 tablespoons curry powder, plus a little extra for garnish
400 g (14 oz) potatoes, diced
500 ml (17 fl oz) vegetable stock
250 ml (9 fl oz) cream
2 tablespoons flat-leaf (Italian) parsley

PREPARE AND COOK THE ARTICHOKES

Cut off and peel the artichoke stems and immediately drop them into a bowl of water with half of the lemon juice added. Remove the artichoke petals and peel them down to the hearts. Also remove the inner petals directly above the artichoke hearts. Immediately drop the petals into the bowl of acidulated water to prevent them from oxidising. Remove and discard the fibrous chokes from the hearts.

Cook the artichoke hearts and stems in boiling salted water for 10–12 minutes. Remove from the saucepan and refresh under cold water. Add the petals to the saucepan and cook until soft, about 25 minutes. Remove the petals from the cooking liquid and blend them to a paste using a stick blender. Pass the paste through a sieve. Strain the cooking liquid through a sieve and reserve 400 ml (14 fl oz).

FINISH THE ARTICHOKE CREAM

Heat the olive oil in a saucepan over medium heat. Add the onion and carrots and sauté briefly. Stir in the curry powder and add the potatoes. Add the vegetable stock, artichoke paste and reserved artichoke cooking liquid. Reduce the heat and simmer the mixture for about 20 minutes. Add the artichoke stems and blend the mixture. Stir the cream into the soup. Slice the artichoke hearts lengthwise and heat them in the soup. Season with salt and a little freshly ground black pepper and serve garnished with parsley and curry powder.

TAPAS BARS

Tapas, or little 'lids' (which is what the words translate as) made of cured meat, ham or bread that were once placed on top of wine glasses to keep bothersome flies out, have developed an amazing life of their own over time. And there is no end in sight to their success story. An entirely new type of restaurant has developed that specialises only in *tapas*. After all, *tapas* is something you can have at any time, as a sit-down meal, on the go or standing at a bar, which is the preferred way by far. Once you start nibbling on these little morsels as an appetiser before your actual dinner, it's all too easy to forget about having a proper meal altogether, as tapas bars are synonymous with a lively, fun-filled atmosphere that makes it difficult to leave.

TAPAS
€1

Bastaix BAR DE VINS, TAPES I COPES

TARTAR DEL DIA

VINS

TAPAS

Peix de mercat

CREMA DE MONGETES

CREMA DE ALUBIAS | CREAMED CANNELLINI BEANS

Legumes have always played an important role in Spanish cuisine and, luckily for us, they have never been quite relegated from this role. This recipe uses canned white beans. If you prefer to use dried beans, make sure you soak them overnight first. I like using a flavourful chicken stock, but this tasty dish can also be prepared with vegetarian stock. These creamed beans can be served as a starter or main course.

Serves 8 | **Preparation:** 10 minutes | **Cooking time:** 20 minutes

2 x 400 g (14 oz) cans
  cannellini beans
100 ml (3½ fl oz) strong
  chicken stock (or vegetable
  stock)
100 ml (3½ fl oz) dry
  white wine
1 small sprig thyme
1–2 tablespoons walnut oil
4 small slices serrano ham,
  oven-dried

Add the beans and their liquid to a small casserole dish. Add a little of the stock and white wine and the sprig of thyme. Cook for 15 minutes over high heat, but be careful not to burn the mixture. Mash the beans with a potato masher.

Remove the thyme and pass the beans through a sieve. Discard any skins remaining in the sieve. Season the resulting cream with more stock and wine, but be careful not to let it get too runny. Add enough walnut oil to give the mixture a creamy consistency. Transfer the mixture to a saucepan and warm over low heat. Serve garnished with pieces of dried ham.

VARIATION

If you make the cream a little thinner and lighter by adding more stock or wine, this makes a flavoursome soup that will serve 4. Alternatively, add more oil to taste to make it a little richer.

SOPA FREDDA AMB ALFABREGA

SOPA FRÍA CON ALBAHACA | CHILLED HERB SOUP

I was once served this chilled Catalan vegetarian soup made according to a recipe by Carme Ruscalleda, one of Barcelona's best-known chefs. It makes a delicious tapa on hot summer days. The ground pine nuts and oil give it a deliciously creamy consistency.

Serves 4–6 | **Preparation:** 25 minutes | **Cooking time:** 30 minutes | **Chilling time:** 1–2 hours

For the vegetable stock
150 g (5½ oz) carrots
150 g (5½ oz) leek
150 g (5½ oz) onions
Olive oil for frying
A few sprigs of parsley,
    finely chopped
1 garlic clove, peeled
2 litres (70 fl oz) boiling
    water

For the herb mixture
100 g (3½ oz) pine nuts
220 ml (7½ fl oz) olive oil
¼ garlic clove
40 g (1½ oz) flat-leaf (Italian)
    parsley, leaves picked
    and chopped
40 g (1½ oz) basil leaves,
    chopped
10 g (¼ oz) salt

PREPARE THE VEGETABLE STOCK
Trim, peel and dice the vegetables. Heat the olive oil for frying in a large saucepan over high heat. Add the vegetables, parsley and garlic clove and sear for 3 minutes. Add the boiling water and simmer everything for about 30 minutes. Season with a little salt and strain through a sieve. Set aside to cool and then refrigerate.

PREPARE THE HERB MIXTURE
Finely grind the pine nuts in a blender, then gradually add the olive oil, blending continuously. Add the garlic and herbs and blend in with some of the strained stock. Add the remaining stock and season with the salt and some freshly ground white pepper. Mix thoroughly. Serve chilled, but not ice cold.

PATATAS AL POBRE

PATATAS AL POBRE | POOR MAN'S POTATOES

Poor man's potatoes are a tasty, rich accompaniment to a wide variety of fish and meat dishes. And often they're delicious enough just by themselves.

Serves 4 | **Cooking time:** 20–25 minutes

200 g (7 oz) onions
400 g (14 oz) waxy potatoes
Olive oil for frying
1 red capsicum (pepper),
  cut into strips
1 green capsicum (pepper),
  cut into strips
1–2 garlic cloves, crushed
2 tablespoons vinegar

Peel and roughly chop the onions. Wash the potatoes thoroughly and slice.

Warm the olive oil in a casserole dish over medium heat. Add the onion pieces and sweat until translucent. Add the potatoes and season with salt. Cook for 12–15 minutes. Add the capsicum strips and garlic, to taste. Continue to cook for another 5–10 minutes. Carefully shake the dish occasionally to prevent the vegetables from burning. Right at the end, add the vinegar and season to taste with more salt.

COCA

COCA | SAVOURY FLATBREADS

Coca is a type of flatbread that is popular all across Catalonia. It originated on the Balearic Isles and is quite similar to pizza. Coca is always made from a yeast dough, which is then topped with vegetables, fish or meat. There are innumerable varieties: square, round and oblong shapes with a thin and crispy or thicker and softer base, with sweet or savoury toppings. Often, coca toppings simply consist of left-over ingredients from the previous day, but there's one thing that NEVER goes on a coca, and that's cheese.

Serves 4 | **Preparation:** 10 minutes | **Marinating time:** 2 hours
Rising time: 40 minutes | **Baking time:** 25 minutes

For the topping
Fresh or dried
   Mediterranean herbs
   (rosemary, bay leaf and,
   above all, thyme)
1 garlic clove, thinly sliced
100 ml (3½ fl oz) olive oil
Red capsicum (pepper),
   peeled or from a jar, cut
   into strips

For the dough
20 g (¾ oz) fresh yeast
1 pinch sugar
500 g (1 lb 2 oz) plain
   (all-purpose) flour
1 teaspoon salt
2 tablespoons olive oil
2 tablespoons white wine
Oil and flour for the
   benchtop and baking tray

PREPARE THE HERB OIL
Marinate the herbs and garlic in the olive oil for 1–2 hours. Remove the garlic, if preferred, or leave in the oil.

PREPARE THE YEAST DOUGH
Dissolve the yeast and sugar in 250 ml (9 fl oz) warm water in a small bowl. Add the flour and salt to a large mixing bowl and make a well in the centre. Pour the dissolved yeast into the well, combine with a little flour to make a starter and leave to rise for 10 minutes at room temperature. Add the olive oil and white wine and combine all ingredients. Knead to make a smooth dough. Cover and set aside to rise in a warm spot until the dough has doubled in volume. This will take about 30 minutes.

BAKE THE COCA
Preheat the oven to 180°C (350°F). Briefly knead the dough once more and roll it out thinly on a surface dusted with flour. Transfer to a baking tray and pierce all over with a fork. Leave to rise for another 10 minutes.

Spread the base generously with the herb oil and herbs. Divide the capsicum evenly over the base and bake the *coca* for 20–25 minutes.

Alternatively, top the base with any tasty combination of blanched spinach, pine nuts and raisins, salt and pepper, or capsicum, onions and cured meats, sardines, tuna or smoked mackerel – there's no limit to your imagination.

OUS FREGITS AMB SAMFAINA

HUEVOS FRITOS CON SAMFAINA | FRIED EGGS ON SAMFAINA

This dish is very easy to make and absolutely delicious, especially for breakfast after a long night out. Basic restaurants often serve it as a starter, but I love it for brunch and often dish it up in two different versions.

Serves 4 | Preparation: 10 minutes

Samfaina (see recipe
   on page 263)
4 eggs
Olive oil
Bread

VERSION 1

The day before, prepare the samfaina according to the recipe. Reheat in a saucepan.

Fry 1 egg per person in a frying pan with olive oil. Keep dousing the egg with the hot oil to ensure that the egg white sets and the egg yolk stays runny.

Lift the egg from the oil. Allow excess oil to drain. Season with salt and freshly ground black pepper and serve in a bowl on top of the samfaina. Serve with bread.

I LIKE VERSION 2 EVEN BETTER!

Reheat the samfaina in a ceramic casserole dish over medium heat. It shouldn't be too thick: thin with a splash of white wine, if necessary. Gently slide 1 very fresh egg per person into the boiling samfaina and poach. The eggs are ready once the egg whites have set and the yolks are still runny. Serve with a slice of toasted bread for breakfast.

TRUITA DE PATATES

TORTILLA DE PATATAS | POTATO TORTILLA

Tortillas are classics of Spanish cooking that are also very popular in Barcelona. They only require very few ingredients, are easy to prepare and always taste delicious.

Serves 4 | **Preparation:** 10 minutes | **Resting time:** 1 hour | **Cooking time:** 40 minutes

800 g (1 lb 12 oz) potatoes
2–3 onions
125 ml (4 fl oz) olive oil
6 eggs

Peel the potatoes and onions. Cut the potatoes into small dice or thin slices and dice the onions finely.

Heat 4 tablespoons of the olive oil in a frying pan over medium heat. Add the potatoes and onions and cook for about 20–25 minutes. Do not allow them to brown.

Season the mixture with salt and freshly ground black pepper and transfer to a large bowl. Whisk the eggs and combine with the potatoes. Set aside to rest for about 1 hour.

Heat the remaining olive oil in the pan over medium heat. Add the potato mixture and cook until set, about 5–8 minutes. Turn the tortilla and cook the other side.

Tortillas can be eaten warm or cold. Slice into wedges or cut into tapas-sized cubes for serving.

TRUITA D'ESPÀRRECS

TORTILLA DE ESPARRAGOS | WILD ASPARAGUS TORTILLA

Once the days get noticeably longer again around the middle or end of January and there has been plenty of rain, people often come home from walks with large bunches of wild asparagus, which grows everywhere around Barcelona. It is a lot more aromatic and flavoursome than the cultivated green asparagus commonly available from shops. Wild asparagus is just fabulous in a tortilla. Unfortunately wild asparagus can be difficult to get in Australia, but standard green asparagus will do just fine.

Serves 4 | **Preparation:** 15 minutes | **Cooking time:** 10 minutes

1 bunch wild asparagus
(or thin green asparagus)
6 eggs
Olive oil
1 onion, finely diced
1 small garlic clove, crushed

Wash the asparagus. Trim off the hard ends and slice the asparagus diagonally into short segments. Whisk the eggs together.

Heat the olive oil in a frying pan over high heat. Add the asparagus, onion and garlic and fry for about 5 minutes. Season with salt and drain on paper towel.

Transfer the fried vegetables to a bowl and combine with the eggs. Reheat the pan with a little oil over low heat. Return the mixture to the pan and cook until set. Flip over and cook the other side. This *truita d'espàrrecs* tastes great at any time of the day, warm or cold.

TRUITA CATALANA AL ESTIL DE LA YAYA

TORTILLA A LA CATALANA DE LA ABUELA | GRANDMA'S TORTILLA

Grandma's truita catalana *is yet another version of tortilla, but quite a bit richer. It is not often found on restaurant menus, as it involves a little more work, but it's definitely worth it!*

Serves 4 | **Preparation:** 10 minutes | **Cooking time:** 25 minutes

1 can white beans
(mongetes/alubias), about
500 g (1 lb 2 oz)
1 piece of air-dried meat
or smoked bacon, about
12 x 1 cm (4½ x ½ inch),
cut into small pieces
1 piece raw sausage,
preferably butifarra, about
10 cm (4 inches) long, cut
into 5–7 pieces
5 very fresh eggs
2 tablespoons olive oil, plus
extra for drizzling
Tomatoes to taste as a
side dish

Drain the beans through a sieve. Heat a frying pan over high heat. Add the drained beans, dried meat and sausage and sweat briefly. Whisk the eggs in a bowl, then stir in the beans and meat, together with a little salt. Stir carefully to combine.

Heat the olive oil in a frying pan. Add the egg mixture and move it around carefully with a wooden spoon until set. As soon as the tortilla is golden-brown on one side, flip it over using a plate and cook it on the other side.

Serve the tortilla lukewarm, together with sliced or quartered tomatoes and a little best-quality olive oil, preferably made from arbequina olives.

XATÓ

XATÓ | ENDIVE AND FISH SALAD

Restaurants once served xató *only during the new wine season, but today this popular dish is available year round. It originally comes from the towns of Sitges, Vilanova and Vilafranca south-west of Barcelona. This delicate, rich salad is very refreshing in the late summer months. The name of the dish is said to come from a French artist, who is said to have exclaimed, 'Mais c'est un Château!' ('It's a castle!') when he was served this dish, piled high on its plate, some time in the late 19th century. Today, so-called* xatónades *are held in the region south-west of Barcelona, where chefs compete for awards for the best* xató *recipes.*

Serves 4 | **Preparation:** 10 minutes

1 large head curly
   endive lettuce
16 anchovy fillets
400 g (14 oz) bacalao (salt
   cod), desalted, cut into
   bite-sized pieces
180 g (6 oz) can tuna
200 g (7 oz) olives,
   drained (preferably
   arbequina olives)
200 ml (7 fl oz) romesco
   sauce (see recipe on
   page 261)

Divide the endive among four plates. Top with 4 anchovy fillets each, pieces of bacalao, tuna and olives. Serve drizzled with romesco sauce.

AMANIDA DE TOMÀQUET I ESPÀRRECS

ENSALADA TIBIA DE TOMATE Y ESPARRAGOS | WARM SALAD OF TOMATOES AND ASPARAGUS

The Baix Llobregat region produces tomatoes, parsley and a lot of green asparagus, so it isn't surprising to find a recipe combining these ingredients. This salad makes a vitamin-rich accompaniment to many summer dishes.

Serves 4 | **Preparation:** 20 minutes | **Cooking time:** 5 minutes

1 bunch green asparagus
6 ripe tomatoes
Vinegar
Olive oil
1 pinch sugar
1 bunch flat-leaf (Italian) parsley

Trim the hard asparagus ends from the asparagus and cut it into pieces about 4 cm (1½ inches) long. Blanch in boiling salted water until just cooked but still firm to the bite.

Meanwhile, cut the tomatoes into bite-sized pieces and toss with a vinaigrette of vinegar, olive oil, salt and sugar.

Pick off the parsley leaves from the stems. Chop coarsely and combine with the tomatoes and vinaigrette.

Drain the asparagus and immediately combine with the tomatoes. Season again to taste and serve warm.

CARGOLS A LA LLAUNA

CARACOLES A LA LLAUNA | BAKED SNAILS

Snails have always been and still are a nuisance in kitchen farmers' gardens, so something needs to be done about them. And what better solution could a true Catalan come up with if not to eat them? This recipe uses banded snails, which are a little smaller than the more expensive and more flavoursome Roman snails.

Serves 4 | **Preparation:** 20 minutes | **Baking time:** 20–25 minutes

800 g (1 lb 12 oz) banded snails (ideally these should not have been fed for 1 week)
Coarse sea salt
Fine sea salt
3 garlic cloves
Olive oil
1 bunch curly parsley, very finely chopped
½ green capsicum (pepper)
Wine vinegar
Romesco sauce for drizzling (see recipe on page 261)
All i oli for dipping (see recipe on page 260)

Preheat the oven to 180°C (350°F). Thoroughly wash the snails in cold water. Cover a baking tray with a layer of coarse sea salt about 3 mm (⅛ inch) thick. Spread the cleaned snails on top of the salt with the shell openings facing upwards. Sprinkle with a little fine salt. Cook on the middle rack of the oven for about 5 minutes.

Reduce the temperature to 160°C (320°F). Peel the garlic. Crush 2 cloves in a mortar and pestle together with a little olive oil and combine with two-thirds of the parsley. Drizzle this mixture over the snails and return the tray to the oven. Bake for another 5 minutes, then sprinkle with freshly ground black pepper and drizzle with olive oil. Return to the oven until the top of the snail meat has turned golden brown.

Meanwhile, finely dice the capsicum and the remaining garlic clove. Combine with olive oil, wine vinegar and a little parsley to make a vinaigrette.

Serve the cooked snails with toasted white bread, the vinaigrette, romesco sauce and *all i oli*, either straight from the baking tray or on a ceramic platter.

A different version of this recipe has the snails covered with about 500 g (1 lb 2 oz) very finely diced tomatoes and a little thyme before they are returned to the oven for the last time.

Many backyards in the old part of town are full of quiet, hidden corners that invite passers-by to have a break over a *caña*, a *copa* and some tapas.

The region around El Prat de Llobregat supplies Barcelona with fresh vegetables all year round, from delicate *calçots* (spring onions/scallions) early in the year to artichokes, broad beans, asparagus and lettuces throughout summer. Later in the year follow potatoes, of course, as well as eggplants (aubergines), tomatoes, capsicums (peppers) and a variety of legumes, all the way through to various cabbages in winter. This is a vegetarian's paradise!

Fish and seafood play a major role in Barcelona, and the seafood section of *La boquería* market has long been a tourist attraction. The variety of fish on offer is huge, as is the price difference between different types of fish. Aquaculture fish such as gilt-head bream and sea bass are cheap, but *peix de la platja*, that is, freshly caught fish, is at least three times as expensive. Still, both the superior quality and taste justify the higher price. Apart from widely known types of fish, you may also come across rarer varieties such as scorpion and weever fish, whose fins have poisonous barbs, which are trimmed off, though, before they are sold.

Poultry has always played an important role in Barcelonian cooking. The traditional regional cuisine works a lot with duck, and farmers in the Garraf district south-east of Barcelona even produce a DO-certified breed of chickens, *pollastre de pota blava*, as well as *pollastre del Penedès* nearby. Sure, the price for a single chicken is multiple times what you might pay for a take-away barbecued chicken, but a single bird will feed a whole family. And in Barcelona's traditional cuisine you'll come across so much more than just chicken: ducks, guinea fowl, partridges and quail also play an important culinary role.

MAIN DISHES

CALÇOTS

CALÇOTS | GRILLED SPRING ONIONS

Calçots originally came from the region around Valls, about 60 kilometres south-west of Barcelona, but these days they are grown and enjoyed all around Barcelona and Tarragona. Local farmers tend to these special spring onions carefully for about a year and plant them tightly so they don't form much of a bulb and mainly greens instead. Calçots are available from December through to late spring. At least once a year, in spring, I simply have to have calçots. I love eating them casually from outdoor stalls with friends; in restaurants, they are often served with grilled meat and vegetables.

Preparation: 30 minutes | **Resting time:** 10 minutes

At least 10 *calçots*
(spring onions/scallions)
per person
Pork cutlets, lamb, blood
pudding, butifarra
Sliced bread
Cannellini beans, artichokes
Plenty of romesco sauce
(see recipe on page 261)

GRILL THE *CALÇOTS*, MAINS AND BREAD
Grill the *calçots* over an open fire, ideally made with old vine prunings, until the outer skin has blackened. Wrap in newspaper and set aside to rest for about 5–10 minutes.

Barbecue the meat for the main dish and toast the sliced bread on the remaining coals. This dish is commonly served in the form of a meat platter with blood pudding, pork cutlets and lamb, with cannellini beans and artichokes on the side.

ENJOY THE *CALÇOTS*
In Spain, grilled *calçots* are served on terracotta ridge tiles. To eat the *calçots*, carefully hold them at the green tops and peel off any blackened leaves in a downward motion. Dip the delicate, white portion of the bulb into the romesco sauce and eat it with your fingers. This is invariably a messy affair – it's best to toss aside any concerns and just enjoy the experience. Most restaurants hand out aprons to guests as they are served their *calçots*.

CARXOFES I PATATES EN VI BLANC

ALCACHOFAS Y PATATAS AL VINO BIANCO | ARTICHOKES AND POTATOES IN WHITE WINE

Artichokes are all-rounders: They taste delicious both as a side dish and as a main. This artichoke and potato stew is bound to be a favourite, not only among vegetarians.

Serves 4 | **Preparation:** 20 minutes | **Cooking time:** 45 minutes

1 bottle of dry, fruity chardonnay
12 Spanish artichokes
12 potatoes
50 ml (1½ fl oz) olive oil
1 bay leaf
1 tablespoon dried thyme

PREPARE THE ARTICHOKES

Pour the wine into a bowl. Cut off and peel the artichoke stems and immediately drop them into the wine. Remove the artichoke petals, scrape the fibrous chokes from the hearts with a sharp-edged spoon and discard. Drop the hearts into the wine also to prevent oxidation.

COOK THE POTATOES AND ARTICHOKES

Peel the potatoes and cut them into eight chunks each. Heat a large casserole dish over medium heat. Add the olive oil, bay leaf, thyme, salt and freshly ground black pepper followed by the potato chunks and fry briefly. Stir in the wine from the bowl and add the artichoke hearts and stems. Simmer, half-covered, for about 20 minutes. Once the artichokes are done, remove them and set them aside.

Continue to cook the potatoes in the casserole dish, uncovered, until all of the liquid has evaporated. This will take about 20 minutes. Shake the dish occasionally to loosen the potatoes. They will firm up in the wine and retain their shape. Meanwhile, halve the artichoke hearts.

Return the artichoke hearts and stems to the dish once the remaining liquid begins to caramelise. Continue shaking the dish occasionally until the last drop of liquid has evaporated. Serve immediately.

CARXOFES AL FORN

ALCACHOFAS AL HORNO | BAKED ARTICHOKES

Barcelona and its surrounding region are well known for an incredible variety of artichoke dishes. The easiest way to prepare this wholesome, delicious vegetable is to roast it in the oven. Artichokes are quite filling; count one artichoke per person for a starter or three per person for a vegetarian main.

Serves 4 | **Preparation:** 10 minutes | **Baking time:** 1 hour

4 oblong artichokes
  (or 12 if serving as a
  main meal)
1–2 garlic cloves, very
  thinly sliced
Plenty of olive oil
Romesco sauce (see recipe
  on page 261)

Preheat the oven to 230°C (450°F). Trim off the artichoke stems so that they will stay upright in the roasting pan. Bash the artichoke heads once against the benchtop, stem side up, to loosen the petals a little.

Combine the garlic, olive oil, salt and freshly ground white pepper in a small bowl. Place the artichokes on a baking tray or in a roasting pan and pour some of the seasoned oil into the centre of each one. Transfer to the middle rack of the oven and reduce the temperature to 180°C (350°F). The artichokes will take about 45–60 minutes to cook through. Once done, the inner petals can be easily pulled out without taking much of the delicate heart with them.

Artichokes match particularly well with romesco sauce. Pull out the petals, one by one, dip the fleshy part into the sauce and pull the petal through the teeth. Make sure you remove the fibrous chokes before eating the delicate artichoke hearts.

TARTA DE CARXOFES AMB PATATES

PASTEL DE ALCACHOFAS Y PATATAS | ARTICHOKE AND POTATO GRATIN

This recipe for oven-baked Spanish artichokes with potatoes is a hearty, rustic affair that will delight the hearts and palates of all fans of this exquisite vegetable.

Serves 4–6 | **Preparation:** 25 minutes | **Cooking and baking time:** 1¼ hours

12 artichokes
Juice of 1 lemon
1.5 kg (3 lb 5 oz) waxy
  potatoes
1 tablespoon olive oil, plus
  some extra for the tin
1 large onion, diced
1 bunch flat-leaf (Italian)
  parsley, chopped
4 sage leaves, thinly sliced
250 g (9 oz) crème fraîche
2 eggs
200 g (7 oz) grated cheese
  (e.g. emmental)

COOK THE ARTICHOKES AND POTATOES

Cut off and peel the artichoke stems and immediately drop them into a bowl of water with the lemon juice added. Pick off the artichoke petals until you get to the choke and heart. Scrape and discard the fibrous chokes from the hearts with a sharp-edged spoon and immediately drop the hearts into the acidulated water.

Cook the artichoke hearts and stems in salted water for 10–12 minutes, then remove from the cooking liquid and refresh under cold water. Slice the artichoke hearts.

Peel and slice the potatoes. Blanch the potatoes in a pot of boiling salted water for about 5 minutes, then refresh under cold water and drain. Heat a little olive oil in a frying pan over medium heat and briefly sauté the onion.

PREPARE AND BAKE THE GRATIN

Combine the artichoke hearts and stems with the onion, parsley, sage, crème fraîche, eggs and cheese in a bowl. Season with salt and freshly ground black pepper.

Preheat the oven to 180°C (350°F). Brush a springform tin with olive oil. Layer half of the sliced potatoes to cover the bottom and side of the tin. Cover with half of the artichoke and egg mixture, then add another layer of potato and finish with the remaining artichoke and egg mixture. Bake on the middle rack of the preheated oven for 50 minutes. Remove from the oven and leave to cool on a cooling rack. Remove the gratin from the tin and serve. This gratin is delicious served with a rocket (arugula) salad dressed with a herb vinaigrette.

ALBERGÍNES FARCIDES

BERENJENAS RELLENAS | STUFFED EGGPLANTS

The district of Baix Llobregat south-west of Barcelona is the city's kitchen garden. It produces not only broad beans and artichokes, but also excellent tomatoes and eggplants. Eggplants are another vegetable that can be prepared in a thousand and one ways. These stuffed eggplants are one of my favourite dishes, but unfortunately they have fallen a little out of fashion, even though they are very easy to prepare.

Serves 4 | **Preparation:** 15 minutes | **Cooking and baking time:** 40 minutes

4 large eggplants
  (aubergines)
1 tablespoon olive oil
1 small red capsicum
  (pepper), finely diced
300 g (10½ oz) mixed
  minced (ground) meat
1 onion, finely diced
1 large, ripe tomato, diced
½ teaspoon ground
  cinnamon
Freshly ground nutmeg
1 tablespoon mild paprika
200 g (7 oz) grated
  emmental cheese

PREPARE THE EGGPLANTS

Preheat the oven to 180°C (350°F). Halve the eggplants lengthwise, leaving the stem base intact, and score the flesh in a diamond pattern. Place the eggplant halves in an ovenproof dish, cut side up, and bake on the middle rack of the preheated oven for 20 minutes. Remove from the oven and carefully scoop out the flesh, making sure the skin remains intact.

Transfer the eggplant flesh to a bowl, mash coarsely and set aside. Reduce the oven temperature to 150°C (300°F).

PREPARE THE FILLING AND BAKE THE EGGPLANT

Heat a little olive oil in a frying pan over medium heat and sear the capsicum. Once it begins to soften, add the minced meat and onion. Continue to fry until browned. Add the tomato and season with cinnamon, nutmeg, paprika, salt and freshly ground black pepper. Simmer until almost all of the liquid has evaporated, then fold in the mashed eggplant flesh.

Fill the eggplant halves with the minced meat mixture and sprinkle with the cheese. Bake on the middle rack of the oven for 10–15 minutes until the cheese is golden brown and bubbling.

ALBERGÍNES AMB TORTA DEL CASAR

BERENJENAS CON TORTA DEL CASAR | BAKED EGGPLANTS WITH TORTA DEL CASAR

Spain has relatively few types of unpasteurised cheese that have real character, but one of them is Torta del Casar from the Extremadura region. This cheese turns very soft as it matures and is then scooped out of the wheel with spoons. I was once served this cheese in Barcelona as part of the dish in the recipe below, which I find thoroughly delectable.

Serves 4 | **Preparation:** 10 minutes | **Frying and baking time:** 15 minutes

4 medium-sized, relatively slender eggplants (aubergines)
1 tablespoon olive oil
1 Torta del Casar (from specialist suppliers or ordered online; alternatively another full-flavoured soft cheese, e.g. Epoisses de Bourgogne)
4 slices of white bread, toasted

Preheat the oven to 180°C (350°F). Trim the stem bases off the eggplants and quarter the vegetables lengthwise. Halve the quarters again. Sprinkle the eggplant pieces with a little salt and set them aside to draw out some of their moisture. Pat dry. Heat an ovenproof pan over high heat and briefly sear the eggplant pieces in the olive oil, then transfer to the oven and cook until done.

Have a ripe Torta del Casar ready at room temperature. Score the top crosswise and then fold back the top segments. Serve the eggplant, cheese and toast on a platter with a spoon for the cheese.

FAVES A LA CATALANA

HABAS A LA CATALANA | CATALAN BROAD BEANS

Broad beans are among the oldest legumes in European cooking, and apparently even the Ancient Egyptians relied on them in their diet. They are also a staple of traditional Spanish cuisine. The Baix Llobregat region produces habas and faves of the highest quality. As just about anything else, broad beans also taste best fresh. If you prefer your culinary adventures to be effortless, simply buy broad beans shelled and ready to cook so you don't have to shell them yourself. This is more expensive, of course, but luckily broad beans are also available canned or frozen. This is a very typical Barcelonian dish that proves yet again that hearty home cooking is often among the very best.

Serves 4 | Preparation: 10 minutes | **Cooking time:** 1 hour 25 minutes

1 dash olive oil
100 g (3½ oz) thickly sliced smoked ham, coarsely chopped
1 garlic clove, crushed
1 slice serrano ham or other dry-cured ham
1 onion, finely diced
1 small sprig rosemary
2 bay leaves
3 ripe tomatoes, seeded and coarsely diced
50 ml (1½ fl oz) dry sherry or dry red wine
1 tablespoon aniseed spirit
750 g (1 lb 10 oz) fresh shelled or canned broad beans
1 large sprig mint, leaves torn
100 ml (3½ fl oz) meat stock
100 g (3½ oz) botifarra blanca or another sausage for frying
100 g (3½ oz) botifarra negra or a mild black pudding

Heat the olive oil in a deep frying pan over high heat and fry the smoked ham and garlic until golden brown. Add the serrano ham and onion and continue to fry, stirring. Add the rosemary and bay leaves and fry for another 3–4 minutes.

Stir in the tomatoes, cover and simmer for 7–8 minutes. Add the sherry and aniseed spirit, then lower the heat and simmer until the sauce reduces and gradually darkens in colour. Fold in the broad beans and torn mint leaves. Add enough stock and water to just cover everything. Season with salt and braise over low heat for 40 minutes.

Slice the sausages 1 cm (½ inch) thick and add to the sauce. Season again with salt and cook, uncovered, for another 15–20 minutes. Remove the herb sprigs and serve in a warmed ceramic bowl.

ESPINACS A LA CATALANA

ESPINACAS A LA CATALANA | SPINACH WITH RAISINS AND PINE NUTS

Espinacs a la catalana, *spinach with raisins and pine nuts, is a true culinary winner. In some restaurants, this delicious dish is also served under the name of* espinacs con pasas y piñones.

Serves 4 | **Preparation:** 10 minutes | **Cooking time:** 15 minutes

2 tablespons raisins, soaked
  in water
750 g (1 lb 10 oz) baby
  English spinach
4 tablespoons olive oil
2 tablespoons pine nuts
1 small garlic clove, halved

Drain the raisins. Wash and drain the baby spinach. Transfer the damp leaves to a large pot and cover with a lid. Cook over high heat for 2–3 minutes until the spinach has collapsed. Leave to cool, then squeeze out the excess moisture and chop finely.

Heat a large pan over medium heat. Add the olive oil, pine nuts and garlic and fry until the nuts start to colour. Shake the pan frequently to prevent them from burning. Remove the garlic. Add the raisins and spinach to the pan. Season with salt and freshly ground black pepper and continue to fry for another 5 minutes, stirring occasionally. Serve straight from the pan or on small plates. Serve with ham and bread.

TIP
You can, of course, also use frozen spinach for this dish. Simply defrost before using and cook in a little water for a few minutes to soften.

MARKETS

In Barcelona, each quarter has its own market. These markets are where locals shop for fresh fruit and vegetables, fish, poultry and meat, above all. Generally, restaurant chefs are the first to do their shopping in the early mornings. A little later, it's local housewives, and by late morning the markets are flooded with tourists.

Barcelona's most famous market is definitely the Mercat de Sant Josep, better known as *La boquería*, which is renowned for its excellent seafood section. However, more and more stalls on *La boquería* are focusing squarely on tourists, and the market has lost a lot of its inimitable flair as a result – enough to have people thinking aloud about limiting tourist numbers.

A number of the city's other markets have been extensively refurbished or are currently undergoing refurbishment. The Mercat de Santa Caterina in the Born/La Ribera quarter, for example, was completed in 2005, and the Mercat Ninot, which serves the Eixample quarter, in 2015. One of Barcelona's most beautiful markets, the Mercat de Sant Antoni, is currently being restored.

CIGRONS AMB CLOÏSSES

GARBANZOS CON ALMEJAS | CHICKPEAS WITH CLAMS

Chickpeas are incredibly versatile legumes that have found their way into kitchens all over the world, and quite rightly so, as they are both delicious and healthy. People all around the Mediterranean recognised their excellent culinary value early on and created a great variety of chickpea recipes. In Spain, pre-cooked chickpeas are available in bulk from butchers, or people simply buy them canned from supermarkets.

Serves 4 | **Preparation:** 10 minutes | **Cooking time:** 35 minutes | **Soaking time:** 4–5 hours

250 g (9 oz) clams (vongole)
Olive oil for frying
1 small garlic clove, crushed
½ teaspoon cayenne pepper
1 onion, diced
2 carrots, diced
1 pinch sweet paprika
1 tablespoon plain
  (all-purpose) flour
1 small glass white wine
300 g (10½ oz) canned
  chickpeas, drained
500 ml (17 fl oz) vegetable
  stock
Flat-leaf (Italian) parsley,
  chopped, for garnish
Chives, chopped, for garnish
1 small red chilli, sliced
  into rings

Place the clams in cold salted water – use 50 g (1¾ oz) salt per 1 litre (35 fl oz) water) – for 4–5 hours to make sure they excrete any sand and other impurities.

Heat a large pan over medium heat. Add the olive oil and garlic and fry gently. As soon as the garlic starts to colour, season with cayenne pepper and add the onion and carrots. Cook until the vegetables are soft, about 10 minutes, then dust with paprika and flour. Deglaze with the wine and allow some of the liquid to evaporate. Add the chickpeas and vegetable stock. Simmer again for a few minutes until almost all of the liquid has been absorbed by the chickpeas.

Heat another pan over high heat. Add olive oil and the drained clams, cover and cook until the clams have opened. Discard any clams that remain closed.

Add the clams to the vegetables, simmer everything for another 5 minutes and season with salt and freshly ground black pepper. Sprinkle with some parsley, chives and chilli for garnish and serve.

AMANIDA DE CIGRONS

GARBANZOS ALIÑADOS | CHICKPEA SALAD

Cooked chickpeas are incredibly versatile: they are excellent in warming stews or as a side dish, and cold chickpeas provide a substantial and delicious base for refreshing summer salads.

Serves 4 | Preparation: 15 minutes

1 mild onion, finely diced
1 Lebanese (short)
  cucumber, peeled
  and finely diced
1 green or red capsicum
  (pepper), seeded and
  finely diced
1 carrot, cooked, finely diced
1 hard-boiled egg,
  finely diced
500 g (1 lb 2 oz) canned
  chickpeas, drained
240 g (8½ oz) can corn,
  drained
Vinegar
Olive oil

Combine the onion, cucumber, capsicum, carrot and egg in a large bowl and fold in the chickpeas and corn. Dress the salad with a vinaigrette prepared from vinegar, olive oil and salt.

TIP
Chickpeas taste even better if they are freshly cooked. Soak dried chickpeas overnight in plenty of water with a little added bicarbonate of soda (baking soda) for 24 hours. (As a guide, use 1 tablespoon bicarbonate of soda per 300 g/10½ oz dried chickpeas.) The next day, boil the soaked chickpeas for about 1 hour, skimming off any scum forming on the surface. Drain well before use.

POTATGE DE CIGRONS AMB CHORIZO

POTAJE DE GARBANZOS CON CHORIZO | CHICKPEA STEW WITH CHORIZO

This stew is eaten all over Spain, with varying ingredients, but I prefer this particularly hearty recipe over any others.

Serves 4 | **Preparation:** 10 minutes | **Frying and cooking time:** 30 minutes

Olive oil for frying
200 g (7 oz) chorizo, sliced
1 garlic clove, crushed
1 onion, chopped
1 carrot, sliced
1 red capsicum
  (pepper), diced
1 green capsicum
  (pepper), diced
600 g (1 lb 5 oz) canned
  chickpeas, drained
1 potato, finely diced
1 tomato, peeled, seeded
  and finely diced
1–3 bay leaves

Heat a large saucepan over medium heat, add the olive oil and fry the sliced chorizo. If the chorizo releases a lot of oil, skim some off. Add the garlic and fry briefly, then add the onion, carrot and capsicums. Cook over low heat until soft, then season with salt and freshly ground black pepper. Add water until it comes up about 2 fingers wide. Bring to the boil, add the chickpeas and increase the heat again.

As soon as the stew returns to the boil, add the potato, tomato and bay leaves. Increase the heat to high and cover to return to the boil, then reduce the heat again and simmer until the potato and chickpeas are cooked through. Season once more with salt and serve.

MONGETES SEQUES AMB BOTIFARRA

ALUBIAS CON BUTIFARRA | BEANS WITH BOTIFARRA

Common beans were introduced to Catalonia in the 16th century and soon became a very popular crop. They could be cooked fresh and, more importantly, could also be dried and stored over extended periods. Botifarra is a type of fresh sausage for frying, which has a high content of lean meat, often even fillet meat. The earliest written record of this very popular dish dates back to 1830. The sausages taste even better barbecued; in this case, simply fry the beans in olive oil with a little diced bacon.

Serves 4 | **Preparation:** 10 minutes | **Cooking time:** 15 minutes

4 fresh botifarra sausages
Olive oil for frying
600 g (1 lb 5 oz) canned
  cannellini beans, drained

For the *picada*
Flat-leaf (Italian) parsley,
  finely chopped
1 garlic clove, crushed
Olive oil

FRY THE SAUSAGES AND BEANS

Prick the sausages with a fork all over to prevent them from bursting while you fry them. Sear the sausages in olive oil in a large pan over high heat. Reduce the heat to cook the sausages until done. Remove them from the pan, reserving the fat in the pan, and keep them warm.

Fry the beans in the reserved fat over high heat until they start to colour. Season with salt and freshly ground black pepper. Return the sausages to the pan for the last few minutes of cooking to reheat.

PREPARE A *PICADA*

Combine the parsley and garlic with a little olive oil to make a *picada* sauce. Drizzle the sauce over the beans to serve.

9.90 €

HAVARTI BARRA
Especial sandwich
Sabor: suau.
Liet: vaca.
Origen: Dinamarca.
Mat. Grasa 60%
9.90 €

♥ Sólo 6% de Grasa Saturada
♥ 75% menos de Colesterol
♥ Sin Lactosa
♥ Sin Gluten

TRENTA
GOUDA VEGETAL.
SENSE LACTOSA
16.90 €

GOUDA TENDRE
Sabor: Suau.
Liet: Vaca.
Origen: Holanda.
Mat. Grasa 45%
8.90 €

BOLA SEMISEC
Sabor: Gustós.
Liet: Vaca.
Origen: Holanda.
Mat. Grasa 45%
10.90 €

BOLA SEC
Sabor: Intens
Liet: Vaca.
Origen: Holanda.
Mat. Grasa 45%
11.90 €

BOLA TENDRE
Sabor: Suau.
Liet: Vaca.
Origen: Holanda.
Mat. Grasa 45%
8.90 €

MANTEGA DEL CADÍ
Absolutament pura
11.90 €

EntreMont

You won't find the enormous variety of cheeses in Barcelona that you have in Paris, but it's worth scouting local shops and markets for some cheese specialties in addition to standard varieties.

PATATES I SOBRASSADA

PATATAS Y SOBRASSADA | MASHED POTATOES WITH SOBRASSADA

Potatoes with sobrassada originated as a peasant dish from Mallorca. Sobrassada is a typically Mallorcan spreadable sausage made out of smoked pork. I was once served this dish, prepared particularly exquisitely, as a first course in the 'La Semproniana' restaurant, and I love cooking it as a surprise for my guests at home.

Serves 4 | **Preparation:** 15 minutes | **Cooking time:** 25 minutes

800 g (1 lb 12 oz) floury potatoes
150–200 ml (5–7 fl oz) lukewarm milk
40 g (1½ oz) butter
Freshly ground nutmeg
1 tablespoon finely chopped herbs to taste, such as basil, flat-leaf (Italian) parsley and coriander (cilantro)
200 ml (7 fl oz) cream
150 g (5½ oz) parmesan cheese, grated
4 slices sobrassada, skin removed, about 2 cm (¾ inch) thick and 6 cm (2½ inches) in diameter
Left-over gravy to taste

PREPARE THE MASHED POTATOES AND SAUCE

Peel the potatoes and boil them in salted water. Drain and combine them with the milk, butter and a pinch of nutmeg. Coarsely mash, fold in the herbs and keep warm.

Heat the cream in a small saucepan over low heat. Add the parmesan to melt.

PUT TOGETHER THE STACKS

Place four 9 cm (3½ inch) ring moulds onto plates and half fill them with hot mashed potatoes. Top with 1 slice of sobrassada each and divide the remaining mashed potatoes among the stacks. Remove the ring moulds and pierce the stacks along the sides at the level of the sobrassada so that its melting red fat drains decoratively onto the plate.

Pour a bed of parmesan sauce around the stack and drizzle the stack with the sauce. If you have any left-over gravy from the day before, use it for garnish. Season with a little grated nutmeg.

NÍSCALOS AMB ALL I JULIVERT

ROVELLONS CON AJO Y PEREJIL | RED PINE MUSHROOMS WITH GARLIC AND PARSLEY

In Catalonia, the mushroom season starts some time in late summer, depending on the weather. The region's most highly coveted mushrooms are definitely rovellons *or* níscalos, *that is, red pine mushrooms, which are prepared in any number of creative ways. This simple recipe really brings out their unique flavour.*

Serves 4 | **Preparation:** 5 minutes | **Cooking time:** 10 minutes

800 g (1 lb 12 oz) red pine mushrooms (ideally small ones)
1 small garlic clove
2 tablespoons flat-leaf (Italian) parsley leaves
1 small sprig rosemary
4 tablespoons olive oil
Sea salt flakes

Clean the mushrooms with a brush and a damp tea towel. Peel the garlic and chop coarsely, together with the parsley and a few rosemary leaves.

Heat the olive oil in a frying pan over medium heat. Add the mushrooms, fry and season lightly with sea salt. Add the herb mixture once the mushrooms start to colour but are still firm to the bite. Continue to fry briefly. Serve with white bread.

OUS FREGITS AMB OU DE REIG

HUEVOS FRITOS CON ORONJA | FRIED EGGS WITH CAESAR'S MUSHROOMS

*In Catalonia, Caesar's mushrooms, ou de reig, are the undisputed 'kings of mushrooms'.
Caesar's mushrooms (Amanita caesarea) belong to the death cap family, but they are edible,
very much in contrast to most of their relatives. Unfortunately they are not commonly available
in stores, despite being among the best edible mushrooms around. If you ever find Caesar's
mushrooms on a menu, make sure not to miss the experience. I was once lucky enough to enjoy
them in a very simple, yet truly regal and exquisitely delicious dish served at the 'Dos Cielos'
restaurant in Barcelona: fried eggs with Caesar's mushrooms.*

Serves 4 | **Preparation:** 10 minutes | **Cooking time:** 15 minutes

400 g (14 oz) Caesar's
mushrooms
Olive oil for frying
60 g (2¼ oz) French shallots,
finely diced
50 ml (1½ fl oz) chicken stock
8 eggs
Shaved manchego cheese
Chopped chives

Clean the mushrooms with a brush and a damp tea towel. If the
mushrooms are large, peel off their orange skins and halve them.
If the caps are still closed, only remove the white outer skin and
also halve the mushrooms.

Heat a little olive oil in a frying pan over medium heat and sauté
the shallots. Add the mushrooms and chicken stock. Season with
salt and freshly ground black pepper and sauté for a few minutes
to reduce the liquid somewhat.

Meanwhile, prepare the fried eggs in another pan, making
sure that the egg yolks remain runny. Transfer 2 fried eggs onto
each plate and season with salt and pepper. Top with the cooked
mushrooms. Garnish with shaved manchego cheese and chives and
drizzle with the bright yellow mushroom juices from the pan.

RAVIOLI DE BOLETS

RAVIOLI DE SETAS | MUSHROOM RAVIOLI

Lorenç Patràs' market stall is right at the front of La boquería *market. In Barcelona, Lorenç is THE expert for anything to do with mushrooms, and his stall is where most restaurants and mushroom aficionados do their shopping. Lorenç organises a private cooking competition among his customers every year, and this winning recipe astounded even him.*

Serves 4 | **Preparation:** 30 minutes | **Frying and cooking time:** 20 minutes

1 kg (2 lb 4 oz) mixed
   mushrooms (chanterelles,
   black chanterelles, red
   pine mushrooms etc.)
Olive oil for frying
1 small garlic clove,
   chopped
1 small piece fresh ginger,
   about 4 cm (1½ inches),
   finely minced
4–5 sage leaves,
   thinly sliced
1 chorizo criollo sausage,
   skin removed
1 egg
Breadcrumbs
4 tablespoons grated
   parmesan cheese
Plain (all-purpose) flour
   for dusting
300 g (10½ oz) pasta dough,
   made from durum wheat
   semolina
60 g (2¼ oz) butter
Flat-leaf (Italian) parsley
   for garnish

PREPARE THE FILLING

Clean the mushrooms with a brush and a damp tea towel and coarsely chop. Heat the olive oil in a large pan or a wok over medium heat. Add the chopped garlic and fry until golden brown, but be careful not to burn it. Add the ginger and mushrooms. Season with three-quarters of the sage and a little salt. Allow any liquid to evaporate. Remove the pan from the heat and set aside to cool. Remove the mushroom mixture from the pan and chop finely. Set aside a quarter of the mushroom mixture.

Shred or chop the sausage and fry in the same pan over medium heat. Transfer to a bowl and add the remaining mushroom mixture, egg, some breadcrumbs and half the parmesan. Mix to combine.

PREPARE THE RAVIOLI

Dust your workbench with flour and roll out the pasta dough into two thin sheets.

Use a tablespoon to divide the filling across one of the pasta sheets, leaving about 6 cm (2½ inches) in between portions. Moisten the dough with water around the filling and place the second sheet on top. Press the two pasta sheets together firmly around the filling. Use a pizza cutter to cut the dough into individual ravioli.

Boil the ravioli in salted water for 3 minutes. They are done as soon as they rise to the top. Drain, divide among serving plates and keep warm.

Gently heat the reserved mushroom mixture in a frying pan with the butter and remaining sage. Divide among the plates with the ravioli. Sprinkle with the remaining parmesan and the parsley and serve.

LLUÇ AMB VERDURETES I OLI DE FONOLL

MERLUZA CON VERDURA Y ACEITE DE HINOJO Y LIMÓN | HAKE WITH JULIENNED VEGETABLES AND HERB OIL

To me, lluç *or* merluza, *that is, hake, tends to be quite boring compared to other fish. But served with fennel, as in this recipe, it suddenly becomes quite exciting.*

Serves 4 | Preparation: 20 minutes **| Cooking time:** 15 minutes

For the herb oil
½ bulb fennel, with fronds
3–4 sprigs dill
4–5 sprigs parsley
½ lemon
1 small cup of olive oil
1 pinch sugar

For the fish fillets
4 hake fillets
Olive oil for frying

For the julienned vegetables
1 eggplant (aubergine)
1 green capsicum (pepper)
1 zucchini (courgette)
1 carrot
Olive oil for frying
½ sprig rosemary, leaves picked off
1 onion, cut into thick rounds

PREPARE THE HERB OIL
Thinly slice the fennel and most of the fronds. Finely chop the dill and parsley. Zest and juice the lemon. Whisk the herbs, lemon zest, a little of the lemon juice and olive oil to a dressing in a bowl. Toss with the fennel and season with sugar and freshly ground black pepper. Leave to marinate at room temperature.

FRY THE HAKE FILLETS
Briefly sear the hake fillets in olive oil in a pan over high heat, flesh side down. Flip over and cook on the skin side. Season with a little salt.

FRY THE JULIENNED VEGETABLES
Wash and trim the eggplant, capsicum, zucchini and carrot. Cut into julienne strips about 5 mm (¼ inch) thick and 4 cm (1½ inches) long. Heat a little olive oil in a pan over high heat and fry the vegetable strips until cooked but still firm to the bite. Season with a little salt and rosemary, then remove from the pan. Fry the onion slices in a little olive oil.

Divide the hake fillets among warmed plates, top with the julienned vegetables and drizzle the fish with the herb oil. Arrange the onion rounds on the side and serve.

LLOBARRO AMB MERMELADA DE CEBA

LUBINA CON MERMELADA DE CEBOLLA | SEA BASS WITH ONION JAM

Freshly caught llobarro *or* lubina, *that is, sea bass, is one of the tastiest fish found in the Mediterranean, as its firm, aromatic flesh makes it a true delicacy. The fillets of a large sea bass, cut horizontally across the back, taste best. The sweetness of the onion jam harmonises fantastically with this aromatic fish, making for an exquisite, yet simple, dish.*

Serves 2 | **Preparation:** 10 minutes | **Cooking time:** 15 minutes

For the onion jam
Olive oil for frying
6 large onions, halved
   and sliced
1 pinch salt
1 tablespoon honey

For the fish fillets
2 large sea bass fillets
Olive oil for frying

PREPARE THE ONION JAM
For the onion jam, heat the olive oil in a large pan over medium heat. Add the onions, fry and season with the salt. Add the honey and keep frying until the onions soften and brown. Keep warm.

FRY THE SEA BASS FILLETS
Pat the fish fillets dry and season lightly with salt and freshly ground black pepper. Heat the olive oil over medium heat in another pan. Briefly sear the fish fillets, flesh side first, then flip over and cook on the skin side.

Arrange the onion jam on top of the fish fillets. Serve with a tomato salad.

RAP A LA MARINERA

RAPE A LA MARINERA | MONKFISH A LA MARINERA

Monkfish look rather grim, despite their name, which would suggest a somewhat more rarefied appearance. However, their boneless, delicate flesh is a sheer delight, and chefs all over Barcelona have come up with a range of highly inventive recipes for preparing this specialty.

Serves 4 | **Preparation:** 25 minutes | **Frying and cooking time:** 40 minutes

Olive oil for frying
1 onion, finely diced
1 garlic clove, thinly sliced
1 red chilli, seeded
  and minced
1 slice white bread, toasted
  and diced
12 blanched almonds,
  finely chopped
4–5 sprigs flat-leaf (Italian)
  parsley, coarsely chopped
125 ml (4 fl oz) white wine
250 ml (9 fl oz) fish stock
  (see recipe on page 261)
6 monkfish or rocklobster
  fillets, about 125 g
  (4½ oz) each
Plain (all-purpose) flour
  for dusting
4 prawns (shrimp)
4 crayfish

Heat the olive oil in a frying pan over high heat. Add the onion, garlic and chilli and sear briefly. Stir in the diced bread, almonds and most of the parsley. Add the white wine and bring everything to the boil. Blend using a stick blender, add the fish stock and briefly return to the boil. Take off the heat and keep warm.

Preheat the oven to 155°C (310°F). Wash the fish, pat dry and season with salt and freshly ground black pepper. Dust the fish fillets in flour and briefly sear in olive oil over medium heat on both sides. Transfer to an ovenproof dish, drizzle with the hot oil from the pan and bake on the middle rack of the preheated oven for 10–15 minutes.

Fry the prawns and crayfish in olive oil for 10 minutes. Arrange on plates together with the fish and the sauce. Garnish with parsley and serve.

BACALAO A LA LLAUNA

BACALAO A LA LLAUNA | BAKED BACALAO

This bacalao recipe, which is very typically Catalan, and particularly Barcelonian, is named after the dish in which it is traditionally prepared. A llauna *is a zinc-coated steel dish about 25 cm (10 inches) square and 4 cm (1½ inches) deep, with handles, that was often used for cooking over open fires. These days,* bacalao a la llauna *is most commonly cooked in a clay casserole dish in a standard oven.*

Serves 4–6 | **Preparation:** 10 minutes | **Frying and baking time:** 35 minutes

800 g (1 lb 12 oz) bacalao
  (salt cod), desalted,
  without skin or bones
50 g (1¾ oz) plain
  (all-purpose) flour
200 ml (7 fl oz) olive oil
3 garlic cloves, thinly sliced
1 tablespoon sweet paprika
1 glass white wine

Preheat the oven to 160°C (320°F). Cut the bacalao into even pieces and dust these in the flour. Heat the olive oil in a frying pan over high heat. Add the fish and sear for 2–3 minutes on each side. Remove from the pan, drain on paper towel and transfer to a clay baking dish.

Fry the garlic in the pan until golden brown. Remove the pan from the heat and stir in the paprika and white wine. Return to medium heat, simmer to reduce, then drizzle the bacalao with the thickened sauce. Transfer to the middle rack of the preheated oven and cook for about 15 minutes until cooked through. Serve with a side salad, cannellini beans or potatoes.

BACALAO AMB CEBA I MEL AL FORN

BACALAO CON CEBOLLA Y MIEL AL HORNO | BAKED BACALAO WITH HONEY AND ONIONS

Honey harmonises perfectly with the salt in the bacalao to deliver a delicately balanced flavour. There is another version of this recipe, where the fish is served with sweet apples.

Serves 4–6 | **Preparation:** 10 minutes | **Frying and baking time:** 35 minutes

50 ml (1½ fl oz) olive oil
3–4 onions, sliced
1 small garlic clove, crushed
2 tablespoons honey
1 kg (2 lb 4 oz) bacalao
  (salt cod), desalted,
  without skin or bones,
  cut into 4–6 pieces
2 tablespoons plain
  (all-purpose) flour,
  plus extra for dusting
40 g (1½ oz) butter
250 ml (9 fl oz) milk
1 pinch freshly ground
  nutmeg

CARAMELISE THE ONIONS

Heat half of the olive oil in a frying pan over medium heat. Add the onions and garlic to sauté. Season lightly with salt. Once the onions start to colour, stir in the honey and caramelise everything for a few minutes.

FRY AND BAKE THE BACALAO

Dust the bacalao in flour and fry over high heat for 2 minutes on each side. Remove from the pan and set aside to drain on paper towel.

Transfer the bacalao to a clay baking dish. Preheat the oven to 180°C (350°F). Prepare a béchamel sauce from the butter, 2 tablespoons flour and milk, season with a little salt and nutmeg and pour on top of the bacalao. Place the baking dish in the oven and immediately reduce the temperature to 150°C (300°F). Bake until done, about 20 minutes. Serve with mashed potatoes and the caramelised onions.

BACALAO AMB SAMFAINA

BACALAO CON SAMFAINA | BACALAO WITH SAMFAINA

Bacalao and samfaina are two very traditional ingredients of Barcelonian cooking.
Combined in a clay dish, they make an excellent pairing of flavours.

Serves 4 | **Preparation:** 15 minutes | **Frying and baking time:** 25 minutes

500 g (1 lb 2 oz) bacalao
(salt cod), desalted,
without skin or bones
3 tablespoons plain
(all-purpose) flour
Olive oil for frying
2 onions, finely diced
2 garlic cloves, crushed
1 red capsicum (pepper),
finely diced
1 green capsicum (pepper),
finely diced
1 large eggplant (aubergine),
finely diced
2 small zucchini
(courgettes), finely diced
2 ripe tomatoes, peeled
and finely diced
Sugar

PREPARE THE BACALAO AND VEGETABLES

Pat the bacalao dry and cut into several small pieces. Dust with flour and fry in olive oil over medium heat until golden brown. Remove from the pan and drain on paper towel.

Add the onions, garlic and capsicums to the same pan, plus extra olive oil if needed, and fry for 5 minutes. Stir in the remaining vegetables and sauté briefly. Deglaze with a little water and season with salt, freshly ground black pepper and sugar.

Return the fish pieces to the pan and cook with the vegetables until everything is done, about 5–10 minutes. Add more water or some fish stock if the pan gets too dry.

Divide the bacalao and samfaina among plates and serve.

LLOBARRO AL FORN AL ESTIL PESCADER

LUBINA AL HORNO AL ESTILO PESCADOR | BAKED SEA BASS, FISHERMAN'S STYLE

Oven-baking is a very traditional way of preparing fish in Barcelona.
The fish best suited for this type of cooking are gilt-head bream and sea bass.

Serves 4 | **Preparation:** 15 minutes | **Frying and baking time:** 35 minutes

1 kg (2 lb 4 oz) potatoes, peeled and sliced
1 onion, thinly sliced
1 bay leaf
200 ml (7 fl oz) olive oil
200 g (7 oz) tomatoes, quartered
1 glass white wine
2 sea bass or gilt-head bream, about 1 kg (2 lb 4 oz) each, kitchen-ready (or 4 fillets)
1 red chilli, thinly sliced into rings
2 garlic cloves, thinly sliced
2 tablespoons vinegar

BAKE THE FISH

Preheat the oven to 160°C (320°F). Place the potatoes, onion and bay leaf into a large baking dish and season with salt and freshly ground black pepper. Drizzle with 100 ml (3½ fl oz) of the olive oil and put on the middle rack of the oven. Once the potatoes are partially cooked after about 10–15 minutes, add the tomatoes and pour in the white wine. Return to the oven and cook until done.

Lightly sear the fish in a non-stick pan over medium heat. Place the fish on top of the baked vegetables and continue to cook in the oven until done.

PREPARE THE SAUCE

For the sauce, heat the remaining olive oil in a pan over medium heat. Add the chilli and garlic and fry until golden brown, then stir in the vinegar. Arrange the fish and vegetables on plates and drizzle with the sauce.

People often queue happily for a table at 'La Paradeta'. Its food comes straight from the market stall into the kitchen.

SALMONETES A LA PARILLA

SALMONETES A LA PARILLA | GRILLED RED MULLET

Both striped red mullet (moll/salmonete de roca) *and red mullet* (moll/salmonete de fang) *are sold at the city's markets, and both are used in a similar manner in Catalan cooking, but striped red mullet is the somewhat preferred fish.*

Serves 4 | **Preparation:** 10 minutes | **Grilling time:** 5 minutes

8 kitchen-ready red mullets
16 sprigs rosemary
2 lemons, halved lengthwise
  and sliced
Olive oil for basting
Coarse sea salt

Preheat the oven on the grill (broiler) setting. Score the skin of each fish several times. Season with salt and stuff with a rosemary sprig and a halved lemon slice each. Place a few slices of lemon and some rosemary on either side of each mullet and hold in place with kitchen twine. Baste the fish with a little olive oil and braise for 5 minutes under the preheated grill. Remove the twine, season with coarse sea salt and serve.

This dish matches perfectly with jacket potatoes served with herb mascarpone or baked potatoes seasoned with rosemary.

CHAMPINIONS AMB MOLL DE FANG

CHAMPIÑONES CON SALMONETES | BUTTON MUSHROOMS
WITH RED MULLET AND SPINACH

*Catalan cooking often matches seafood with ingredients from the hinterland,
especially in the regions along the coast. These combinations are referred
to as* mar i muntanya *– sea and mountains.*

Serves 4 | **Preparation:** 25 minutes | **Frying and baking time:** 25 minutes

8 large button mushrooms
100 g (3½ oz) baby
    English spinach
Olive oil for frying
4 tablespoons cream
Garlic chives, thinly sliced
2 garlic cloves, thinly sliced
6 red mullet fillets
Deep-fried parsley
    for garnish

Preheat the oven to 180°C (350°F). Snap off the mushroom stems
and gently clean the mushroom tops.

Briefly wilt the spinach in a saucepan with a little olive oil over
low heat. Drain on paper towel and chop. Combine the spinach
and cream and season with salt. Fry the garlic chives and garlic in
olive oil until crisp.

Heat an ovenproof pan over medium heat. Add some olive oil
and briefly sear the mushroom tops. Sprinkle the insides with a
little salt and stuff with the spinach mixture. Bake the mushrooms
on the middle rack of the oven until done, about 3 minutes.

Cut the red mullet fillets into even pieces about 5 x 5 cm
(2 x 2 inches). Briefly sear the mullet pieces in a non-stick pan
over high heat on both sides. Season with salt and freshly ground
black pepper.

Assemble two pieces of fish each on the stuffed mushrooms
(use toothpicks to hold them in place). Serve garnished with crispy
fried parsley and the fried chives and garlic.

ESCAMARLANS AMB CREMA DE ALVOCAT

CIGALA CON CREMA DE AGUACATE | NORWAY LOBSTER WITH AVOCADO CREAM

Norway lobster must surely be among the most exquisite seafood around. It is an essential ingredient in any seafood paella or fideua *and is delicious simply served* a la plancha *or barbecued. However, there are also more refined recipes such as the one below, which I once enjoyed in the 'Etapes' restaurant.*

Serves 4 | **Preparation:** 20 minutes | **Cooking time:** 10 minutes | **Chilling time:** 4–5 hours

For the avocado cream
4 ripe avocados
2 tablespoons cream
Juice of 1 lime
4 tablespoons olive oil
1 French shallot, finely diced

For the Norway lobster
1 ripe tomato, peeled, seeded and finely diced
1 green capsicum (pepper), finely diced
1 French shallot, finely diced
4 tablespoons olive oil
1 teaspoon *pimentón de la vera* (semi-hot paprika)
12 Norway lobsters or scampi, about 150 g (5½ oz) each, deveined
Chervil leaves or chopped chives for garnish

PREPARE THE AVOCADO CREAM
Halve the avocados, remove the stones and transfer the flesh to a bowl. Combine with the cream, lime juice, olive oil and shallot and blend until smooth. Season with salt and freshly ground black pepper and freeze or transfer to an ice cream maker for 4–5 hours. Stir every 30 minutes, if possible.

FRY AND PLATE THE NORWAY LOBSTER
Dress the tomato, capsicum and shallot with the olive oil and paprika in a bowl.

Remove the heads of the Norway lobsters. Shell the tails except for the last segment on each lobster and season with salt. Sear in a non-stick pan over medium heat.

Arrange 3 Norway lobsters with a little salad and 1 ball of the iced avocado cream each on plates and serve garnished with chervil leaves or chopped chives.

TIP
If serving this dish as a starter, count only one Norway lobster per person and serve with a leafy salad, for example baby English spinach, baby beetroot and radicchio, instead of vegetables. For a very sophisticated presentation, thinly slice a zucchini lengthwise and roll up to form a ring to hold each lobster as shown.

TELLERINES A LA PLANCHA

COQUINAS A LA PLANCHA | FRIED COCKLES

Even 15 years ago, one would find entire families digging around in the shallows along Barcelona's beaches, all searching for Mediterranean cockles for their lunch or dinner tables. These days, however, this has become a much rarer sight. Cockles a la plancha are an absolute delicacy that couldn't be easier to prepare! In the restaurants along the beach, cockles are often served under the name of tallarines, *but it's best to check before ordering anything by this name, as the same word can also mean 'tagliatelle'.*

Serves 4 | **Preparation:** 10 minutes | **Cooking time:** 10 minutes | **Cockle cleaning time:** 3–4 hours

600 g (1 lb 5 oz) cockles
1 garlic clove, thily sliced
Olive oil
Juice of ½ lemon
Flat-leaf (Italian) parsley,
  chopped, for garnish

If you plan to cook cockles collected from a sandy beach at home, it's best to ensure that they are given enough time to self-clean, as there's nothing more unpleasant than chewing on sand. To do this, immerse the cockles (or any type of mussels) in a bowl of salt water a few hours before you intend to start cooking. Use 50 g (1¾ oz) salt per 1 litre (35 fl oz) water and change the water two or three times.

Clean the cockles as described above, then heat a pan over very high heat and fry the cockles together with the garlic for about 3–4 minutes, covered, so that the shells open. Shake the pan and discard any cockles that have not opened. Add a generous splash of olive oil and the lemon juice. Season with freshly ground white pepper and serve on a platter, garnished with the parsley.

CLOÏSSES AMB BORRATJA

ALMEJAS CON BORRAJAS | CLAMS IN A BORAGE STOCK

Borage grows wild just about everywhere around Barcelona. Elsewhere in Europe, it is cultivated and used as a salad herb or seasoning for cucumber dishes. In the past, borage was not only used as a healing herb, but also prepared as a healthy vegetable of its own, according to a range of creative recipes, and it might just be time for us to remember these old traditions!

Serves 4 | **Preparation:** 15 minutes | **Cooking time:** 20 minutes

300 g (10½ oz) borage
100 ml (3½ fl oz) olive oil
1 garlic clove, crushed
1 heaped tablespoon plain (all-purpose) flour
4 tablespoons white wine
400 g (14 oz) clams, cleaned (see page 154)
4–5 sprigs flat-leaf (Italian) parsley, chopped

Wash the borage and blanch whole (stems and leaves) for about 5 minutes in lightly salted boiling water. Drain, cut into pieces and reserve the cooking liquid.

Heat a pan over low heat, add the olive oil and sauté the garlic, stirring constantly to prevent any browning. Add the flour and sweat briefly. Add the white wine and about 200 ml (7 fl oz) of the borage cooking water. Bring everything to the boil and simmer for 2 minutes. Add the clams to the sauce and continue to cook for another 2 minutes until they open, then add the borage and parsley. Season with salt and freshly ground white pepper. Continue to simmer for 2 minutes and then serve with fresh white bread.

CLOÏSSES A LA MARINERA

ALMEJAS A LA MARINERA | CLAMS IN A HEARTY SAUCE

Cloïsses a la marinera is a delicacy that is available all year round. Virtually all restaurants, especially those directly on the beaches, have this simple, yet entirely delicious, dish on their menus. Fresh clams should be cleaned in salt water before cooking (see page 154).

Serves 4 | **Preparation:** 10 minutes | **Cooking time:** 30 minutes

100 ml (3½ fl oz) white wine
2 bay leaves
500 g (1 lb 2 oz) large or 1 kg
  (2 lb 4 oz) small clams
50 ml (1½ fl oz) olive oil
1 onion, chopped
1 garlic clove, finely minced
1 teaspoon sweet paprika
1 tablespoon plain
  (all-purpose) flour
2 ripe tomatoes, peeled,
  seeded and finely diced
1 small dried red chilli,
  seeded and chopped

Add half of the wine, a little water and the bay leaves to a large pan and heat over very high heat. Add the clams, cover and steam for 3–4 minutes until the shells open. Do this in several batches, if necessary. Remove and discard any shells that do not open. Strain the clam broth through a piece of muslin (cheesecloth) and reserve.

Heat the olive oil in a pan over medium heat. Add the onion and garlic and sauté until golden brown. Reduce the heat. Thoroughly stir in the paprika and flour to form a roux. Continue to simmer for 3–4 minutes, then add the remaining wine and reserved clam broth. Simmer to reduce the liquid. Stir in the tomatoes and dried chilli. Return the clams to the thickened sauce after about 10 minutes. Bring to the boil over high heat and stir well.

Serve with white bread.

Some shops specialise in deli products.

GAMBAS AMB ROMESCO

GAMBAS CON ROMESCO | PRAWNS IN ROMESCO SAUCE

This dish is based on a variation of the traditional
romesco sauce, which imparts a unique flavour.

Serves 4 | **Preparation:** 10 minutes | **Cooking time:** 20 minutes

100 ml (3½ fl oz) olive oil
12–16 large or king prawns (shrimp)
1 garlic clove, thinly sliced
80 g (2¾ oz) almonds, blanched and peeled
1 small onion, diced
2 small red chillies, seeded and minced
3 large ripe tomatoes, peeled, seeded and finely diced
1 bay leaf
4–5 sprigs flat-leaf (Italian) parsley, chopped
1 slice stale white bread, diced
Sherry vinegar

PREPARE THE PRAWNS

Heat a little olive oil in a pan over high heat. Add the prawns to sear, then remove from the pan and set aside.

PREPARE THE ROMESCO SAUCE

Add the garlic and almonds to the pan together with a little olive oil. Fry over high heat until golden brown, then remove from the pan and set aside. Sauté the onion in a little more olive oil until translucent. Add the chillies, tomatoes and bay leaf. Increase the heat and simmer to reduce a little.

Meanwhile, crush the garlic, almonds, parsley and white bread in a mortar and pestle or blend with a stick blender. Add the mixture to the sauce along with a little water and season with salt, freshly ground white pepper and sherry vinegar.

Add the prawns to the hot sauce and simmer gently for a few minutes. Be careful not to allow the sauce to boil.

PAELLA AMB MARISCS

PAELLA DE MARISCOS | SEAFOOD PAELLA

Paella originated in the region around Valencia and Alicante. In the past, it was usually cooked on Thursdays, which was the day before fish and seafood were traditionally bought fresh again from the markets. Paella recipes vary between one region and the next, and recipes differ even between different parts of Barcelona. Try to avoid eating paella on Barcelona's Ramblas — you'll find it better and cheaper in other streets that are less frequented by tourists.

Serves 4–6 | **Preparation:** 25 minutes | **Cooking and frying time:** 40 minutes

200 ml (7 fl oz) olive oil

2 garlic cloves, thinly sliced

2 dried nyora peppers from specialist suppliers or 2 g (1/16 oz) saffron (see tip on page 166)

1 small glass white wine

8 large prawns (shrimp)

4 large Norway lobsters or scampi

1 onion, finely chopped

250 g (9 oz) squid, finely diced

400 g (14 oz) short-grain rice (*arroz bomba*)

3 tomatoes, peeled, seeded and finely diced

1.5 litres (52 fl oz) fish stock (see recipe on page 261)

1 red capsicum (pepper), roasted, peeled and diced

200 g (7 oz) each mussels and clams (vongole), cleaned (see page 154)

PREPARE THE VEGETABLES AND SEAFOOD

Heat a large, deep paella pan or frying pan over high heat. Add a little olive oil and fry the garlic and dried nyora peppers until golden brown. Remove the peppers from the pan and drain well on paper towel. Once cool, crush them to a fine powder in a mortar and pestle. Combine the powder with the white wine and set aside.

Heat a little oil in the pan over high heat. Add the prawns and Norway lobsters and sear all over. Remove from the pan and set aside.

Reduce the heat to medium and add a little more olive oil to the pan, together with the onion. Sauté until translucent, then add the diced squid and sear. Remove from the pan and set aside.

PREPARE THE RICE

Heat the remaining olive oil in the pan, add the rice and sauté over medium heat for 2 minutes. Stir in the tomatoes, 1 litre (35 fl oz) of the fish stock and the wine mixture. Stir in the capsicum and season to taste. Increase the heat to high and boil the rice in the stock for 5 minutes, then reduce the heat again and continue to cook for another 7–8 minutes. Add more fish stock if the rice turns too dry. Season again.

PUT TOGETHER THE PAELLA

Stir the clams into the rice and arrange the remaining seafood decoratively on top, with the mussels around the edge of the pan. Cover the pan and cook over medium heat until done, about 3–4 minutes. Ideally, the rice will start to stick to the pan – the crunchy rice is almost the best thing about a paella. Remove the paella from the heat and leave to rest, covered, for 5 minutes before serving.

ARRÒS DE GALERES AMB CARXOFES

ARROZ CON GALERAS Y ALCACHOFAS | MANTIS SHRIMP AND ARTICHOKES ON RICE

Galeras or mantis shrimp are unusual-looking creatures that are not particularly well known outside Spain, and even here they are mainly used as an ingredient in stocks and soups. This doesn't do them justice, though, as mantis shrimp taste excellent, even though they have relatively little flesh and are quite tricky to shell. If you prefer, you can substitute any other saltwater prawns.

Serves 4 | Preparation: 10 minutes | **Cooking time:** 40 minutes

Olive oil for frying
200 g (7 oz) artichoke hearts (ideally fresh), thinly sliced
1 garlic clove, halved
1 small onion, finely diced
½ green capsicum (pepper), finely diced
16 galeras (mantis shrimp) or other large prawns (shrimp)
500 g (1 lb 2 oz) short-grain rice (arroz bomba)
100 ml (3½ fl oz) white wine
100 ml (3½ fl oz) brandy
3 ripe tomatoes, peeled, seeded and finely diced
2 dried nyora peppers from specialist suppliers or 2 g ($^{1}/_{16}$ oz) saffron (see tip)
1.5 litres (52 fl oz) seafood or fish stock (see recipe on page 261)

Heat a large, deep pan over high heat. Add olive oil, the artichoke hearts and garlic and fry for 5 minutes. Remove from the pan and set aside.

Add 4 tablespoons olive oil to the same pan and sweat the onion and capsicum until translucent over medium heat. Add the shrimp and rice and continue to fry for 5 minutes. Add the white wine, brandy, tomatoes and nyora peppers or saffron. Stir in the stock and season with salt. Simmer for 20 minutes over low heat, returning the artichokes and the garlic to the stock after about 10 minutes. Peel some of the shrimp before serving; fold others in with the rice. Serve garnished with the peeled shrimp.

TIP

Nyora peppers are reddish-black, plum-sized dried peppers with an aromatic, slightly bitter, mildly spicy flavour. If you can get nyora peppers, use them to impart a unique aroma and colour to just about any rice or pasta dish. To prepare, remove the stem base and seeds from 1 nyora pepper. Thinly slice 1 garlic clove. Fry both in hot olive oil until the garlic has turned golden brown, but be careful not to burn the garlic. Reserve the oil for later use and discard the garlic. Drain the pepper and leave to cool. It will have turned brittle. Finely crush the cooled pepper in a mortar and pestle together with a little coarse sea salt. Stir into fish stock; note that you may then be able to reduce other seasonings to taste.

Nyora peppers are sometimes also referred to as Nora chillies. Columbus first brought them back from the New World and left them with monks in the congregation of La Nora in Spain, hence the name.

ARRÒS NEGRE AMB SIPIA

ARROZ NEGRO CON SEPIA | BLACK RICE WITH SQUID

When I first had this dish put in front of me at a table, I had serious doubts whether I'd enjoy it. But be bold: black rice, coloured with squid ink, is a true delicacy. Squid ink is available from good fishmongers, or you can order it online. Or go to Barcelona…

Serves 4 | **Preparation:** 10 minutes | **Cooking time:** 30 minutes

600–750 g (1 lb 5 oz–
　1 lb 10 oz) squid tubes
Olive oil for frying
1 onion, finely diced
1 small garlic clove, crushed
½ red capsicum (pepper),
　finely diced
1 large tomato, peeled,
　seeded and finely diced
1 teaspoon paprika
4 sachets squid ink, about
　4 g (⅛ oz) each
300 g (10½ oz) short-grain
　rice (arroz bomba)
750 ml (26 fl oz) hot fish
　stock (see recipe on
　page 261)

Finely dice the squid tubes. Heat a little olive oil in a large frying pan. Briefly sauté the onion and garlic over medium heat. Add the capsicum, season with salt and continue to cook for about 5 minutes, stirring constantly. Stir in the tomato and continue to simmer for a few more minutes.

Fold in the paprika, squid ink, diced squid and rice. Add the hot fish stock. Increase the heat to high and simmer for 5 minutes. Reduce the heat and simmer for another 13–15 minutes, adding more fish stock if necessary. Once the rice has cooked, remove the pan from the heat. Cover and set aside to rest for a few minutes. Serve with *all i oli* (see page 260).

FIDEOS AMB MARISCS

FIDEOS CON MARISCOS | SEAFOOD FIDEO PASTA

Anyone who believes that Italy is the only true home of pasta is entirely wrong. Catalans have been eating and enjoying pasta for over 500 years – remember that parts of modern-day Italy once belonged to the kingdom of Catalonia. The most popular pasta types are canelones *and* fideos. Fideos *are short, thin semolina vermicelli, which can be prepared in a seemingly endless variety of ways. Feel free to vary the seafood in this recipe to your preference. This is the Catalan response to Valencia's seafood paella.*

Serves 4 | **Preparation:** 10 minutes | **Frying and baking time:** 45 minutes

150 ml (5½ fl oz) olive oil
400 g (14 oz) fideo pasta
No. 1 or another type
of short, thin pasta
1 onion, finely diced
200 g (7 oz) squid
tubes, sliced
1 litre (35 fl oz) hot fish stock
(see recipe on page 261)
200 g (7 oz) clams, cleaned
(see page 154)
8 mussels, cleaned
16 prawns (shrimp), peeled
and deveined

Preheat the oven to 150°C (300°F). Heat the olive oil in an ovenproof pan over medium heat and fry the pasta until golden brown. Once it starts to brown, add the onion and sweat until translucent, stirring constantly. Quickly stir in the squid and fry everything for a few more minutes. Pour in the hot fish stock and simmer over medium heat for 5 minutes, stirring constantly.

Transfer the pan to the middle rack of the oven and bake for 12–15 minutes until all of the liquid has been absorbed. Remove from the oven and add the remaining seafood. Reduce the temperature a little, cover the pan and cook until done, 5–10 minutes.

ARRÒS AMB GAMBES I FONOLL

ARROZ CON GAMBAS Y HINOJO | PRAWNS AND FENNEL ON RICE

Catalans eat many varieties of rice, but their absolute favourite is arroz bomba, *short-grain rice from the Ebro delta, which is commonly used for paella dishes. For this recipe, you can substitute any good Italian risotto rice. Fennel adds a fresh flavour to the dish. I love to use wild fennel, which grows right outside my door here in Barcelona, as it has a much richer aroma.*

Serves 4 | **Preparation:** 20 minutes | **Cooking time:** 1¼ hours

For the *fumet* bouillabaisse
Prawn (shrimp) heads and
  shells, small prawns or
  other shrimp
60 g (2¼ oz) butter
1 garlic clove, thinly sliced
40 g (1½ oz) carrots,
  finely diced
40 g (1½ oz) onions,
  finely diced
¼ bulb fennel, finely diced
150 ml (5½ fl oz) white wine

For the prawns and rice
Olive oil for frying
200 g (7 oz) squid tubes,
  finely diced
1 onion, finely diced
500 g (1 lb 2 oz) large
  prawns (shrimp), peeled
  and deveined
100 g (3½ oz) risotto rice
125 ml (4 fl oz) cream
Fennel or dill fronds
  for garnish

COOK THE *FUMET*
For the fumet bouillabaisse, coarsely mash the prawn heads and shells with the prawns in a mortar and pestle. Heat a saucepan over medium heat. Melt the butter, add the seafood, garlic and vegetables and sauté. Add the white wine and 500 ml (17 fl oz) water. Simmer for 30 minutes, then strain and set aside.

PREPARE THE PRAWNS AND RICE
Heat a little olive oil in a frying pan over medium heat and fry the squid and onion. Set aside the best 4 prawns. Coarsely chop the other prawns and add to the pan. Fold in the rice and sauté everything. Add enough of the strained fumet to cover and simmer for 18–20 minutes, stirring constantly with a wooden spoon. Season with salt and freshly ground white pepper and add the cream right at the end of the cooking time.

Briefly fry the whole prawns in olive oil in another pan. Arrange the rice on plates using ring moulds and top with 1 fried prawn each. Garnish with fennel fronds or dill, carefully pour a bed of *fumet* around the rice and serve.

OSMOSIS

There is certainly no shortage of creativity among Barcelona's chefs and restaurateurs. One of my favourite restaurants, 'Osmosis', has established its own niche in the city's rich culinary scene. It only uses the freshest of ingredients and doesn't even have a store room, as everything comes straight from the market.

Once a week, chef Fredereic Fernandez and his team cook a five-course degustation menu, which is always based around a soup, a rice dish or salad, and fish, followed by poultry or meat and finally dessert. But that's not all: the menu starts off with an amuse-gueule, generally a home-made *foie micuit* (duck or goose foie gras) and finishes with a second dessert that involves chocolate three ways. It's best to leave the choice of wines to the sommelier, who happens to be the co-owner of 'Osmosis'. Here you'll find heaven on a plate!

GUATLLES AMB PEBROTS VERMELLS

CODORNICES CON PIMIENTOS ROJOS ASADOS | QUAIL AND QUAIL EGGS ON MARINATED CAPSICUM

This dish serves up quail in two distinct flavours. Escabeche *is a tasty sauce in which the quail is slowly simmered for an incomparably tender result.*

Serves 4 | **Preparation:** 25 minutes | **Cooking and frying time:** 1¾ hours

For the quail
4 kitchen-ready quails
Soy sauce for the marinade
Olive oil for frying

For the *escabeche*
1 onion, finely diced
1 carrot, finely diced
1 garlic clove, crushed
1 bay leaf
5–6 black peppercorns,
  lightly crushed
150 ml (5 fl oz) olive oil
50 ml (1½ fl oz) sherry
  vinegar
50 ml (1½ fl oz) dry sherry

For the quail eggs
Vinegar
12 fresh quail eggs

For serving
Marinated grilled capsicums
  (see recipe on page 262)

PREPARE THE QUAIL AND *ESCABECHE*
Separate the quail legs, place in a bowl and cover with soy sauce. Leave to marinate while preparing the rest of the dish. Discard the necks and wings, as they are not used in this recipe.

Combine the ingredients for the *escabeche* in a saucepan and heat over medium heat. Add the quail breasts and simmer until soft, about 1½ hours. Season with salt and freshly ground black pepper. Take the quail breasts out of the saucepan and remove the skin and bones. Return the breasts to the *escabeche* to keep warm.

Heat the olive oil in a frying pan over medium heat. Remove the quail legs from the marinade and fry on all sides until done.

POACH THE QUAIL EGGS
Add salt and a dash of vinegar to a pan of water and bring to the boil. Use a wooden spoon to stir the water, creating a whirlpool. Crack the quail eggs open and slide them right into the centre of the whirlpool of boiling water, one by one. As soon as the egg whites have set, lift the poached eggs out of the water with a slotted spoon and refresh them under cold water. Remove any unsightly bits of coagulated egg white.

PLATE THE QUAILS
Remove the quail legs and breasts from the marinade and pan. Score the breasts crosswise. Divide among plates on top of warmed, marinated capsicum strips and arrange the poached eggs on the side.

TIP
For serving, combine 1 teaspoon paprika and 3 teaspoons warmed olive oil. Drizzle the finished dish with the paprika oil and a little balsamic vinegar and serve garnished with flat-leaf (Italian) parsley.

PERDIU ESCABETXADA

ESCABECHE DE PERDIZ | PARTRIDGE IN *ESCABECHE*

Escabeche *is actually a kind of acidic marinade used to preserve fish and meat. The marinated fish or meat is then generally eaten cold or just at room temperature. Partridge in* escabeche *is a very popular dish in Spain. I'm particularly fond of the following version, which is served hot in Barcelona's 'La Pitarra' restaurant. You can substitute the perdices for partridges in this recipe.*

Serves 4 | Preparation: 25 minutes | **Cooking and frying time:** 1 hour 50 minutes
Marinating time: 12 hours

2 large, kitchen-ready
   partridges
1.5 litres (52 fl oz) olive oil
4 onions, finely diced
4–5 garlic cloves, crushed
2 carrots, finely diced
2 turnips, peeled and
   quartered
250 ml (9 fl oz) fino sherry
250 ml (9 fl oz) chicken
   stock
2 tablespoons black
   peppercorns
1 bay leaf
1 sprig thyme

BRAISE THE PARTRIDGES

Tie the partridge legs and wings to the body with kitchen twine and season the birds with salt and freshly ground black pepper. Heat a roasting pan over medium heat. Add a little olive oil and fry the birds until browned all over. Add the remaining ingredients and cook everything over low heat for at least 1½ hours.

Leave to cool, then refrigerate and marinate in the stock for 1 day.

PLATE THE PARTRIDGES

Halve the birds and carefully trim the meat off the bones. Reheat the meat in the stock. Remove from the stock and divide among plates. This goes well with *samfaina* (see page 263), *patatas al pobre* (see page 74) or mashed potatoes.

COLOMAS AMB POCHAS

PICHONES CON POCHAS | PIGEON WITH CANNELLINI BEANS

Spaniards eat a lot of poultry in general, and the local pigeons and partridges are among the finest you'll ever find in restaurants. The beans in the original recipe are Spanish pochas *beans — white beans that are harvested before they are fully ripe. You can substitute alubia beans (available from specialist suppliers) for cannellini beans, which you'll find anywhere.*

Serves 4 | **Preparation:** 25 minutes | **Frying and cooking time:** 1¼ hours

For the poultry
4 kitchen-ready young
   pigeons or 2 partridges
40 g (1½ oz) lard
50 ml (1½ fl oz) olive oil
1 carrot, finely diced
1 small garlic clove, very
   finely crushed
5–6 sprigs flat-leaf (Italian)
   parsley, finely chopped
1 small glass brandy
150 ml (5 fl oz) meat stock

For the sauce
250 g (9 oz) young
   white beans
1 onion, diced
1 green capsicum
   (pepper), diced
3 fully ripe tomatoes,
   peeled, seeded and diced
Olive oil for frying
50 g (1¾ oz) serrano ham,
   finely diced

PREPARE THE POULTRY
Generously season the pigeons with salt. Heat the lard and olive oil in a casserole dish over medium heat. Add the pigeons, carrot, garlic and about half of the parsley and deglaze with the brandy. Cook over very low heat until the liquid has evaporated. Add the stock and continue to simmer for another 20 minutes. Add more stock if necessary.

PREPARE THE BEANS AND VEGETABLES
Meanwhile, cover the beans with water in a saucepan and simmer over medium heat until soft, about 20 minutes. Season with a little salt.

Fry the onion, capsicum and tomatoes in olive oil in a frying pan over medium heat. Cook for 20 minutes, then blend with a stick blender. Combine with the beans in the saucepan, add the diced ham and simmer everything for another 20 minutes.

Transfer the bean mixture to the casserole with the pigeons and cook until heated through. Garnish with the remaining parsley and serve in the casserole dish.

TIP
If you want to serve this dish as a starter, don't prepare it as a stew, but instead arrange the pigeons and sauce decoratively on plates, garnished with chives. Serve the beans separately and reduce the quantity of beans accordingly.

Barcelonian markets are treasure troves of exquisite ingredients and delights.

POLLASTRE FARCIT

POLLO RELLENO | STUFFED ROAST CHICKEN

This 'Sunday roast' is worth every minute of time and every cent of money necessary to get it onto the table as deliciously as possible. I therefore recommend using only the best ingredients, above all a chicken of superior quality. It's best to have the chicken fully deboned by a butcher so you can focus on the stuffing. Ask your butcher to also remove the tips of the wings, but to leave the chicken body intact.

Serves 4 | **Preparation:** 30 minutes | **Cooking and frying time:** 1 hour 10 minutes
Resting time: 12 hours

1 kitchen-ready chicken for roasting
1 fresh, lean botifarra, cut into pieces
3–4 slices edam or emmental cheese
3–4 slices bacon
1 small jar of pimientos del piquillo
2–3 hard-boiled eggs, quartered
8 olives, pitted
200 g (7 oz) fresh red pine mushrooms, cleaned, or 150 g (5½ oz) mushrooms from a jar, drained
Olive oil for frying
4–5 onions, diced
2 tablespoons almonds and hazelnuts, coarsely chopped
1 chicken or vegetable stock cube
600 ml (21 fl oz) beer

STUFF AND SEAR THE CHICKEN

Spread the chicken flat on your workbench. Season the inside with salt and freshly ground black pepper. Spread with botifarra and top with the sliced cheese, bacon, pimientos, eggs, olives and a good third of the mushrooms. Roll up like a Swiss roll and tie together firmly with kitchen twine so that the stuffing cannot fall out.

Heat some olive oil in a roasting pan over high heat and fry the onions. Add the stuffed chicken and fry on all sides. Keep loosening it from the pan to prevent it from burning.

COOK THE CHICKEN IN THE SAUCE

Add the chopped almonds and hazelnuts, the crumbled stock cube and the remaining mushrooms and deglaze with the beer. Bring to the boil over high heat, then reduce the heat and continue to simmer the chicken. The chicken is cooked when no liquid escapes from the meat when it is pierced with a wooden skewer.

Leave the chicken to cool in the stock and then allow to rest overnight. The next day, slice the cold chicken and return it to the gravy. Reheat in a hot oven and serve.

POLLASTRE AMB ESCAMARLANS

POLLO CON CIGALAS | CHICKEN WITH SEAFOOD

Catalans have a special name for dishes that combine seafood with meat, poultry or vegetables from the hinterland: mar i muntanya *– sea and mountain, and these recipes are very distinctively Catalan.* Mar i muntanya *food is the product of Catalan chefs' innovative and adventurous approach to their craft. Do try them – I promise you'll be rewarded with many pleasant surprises. By the way, chocolate has been used in Catalan cooking since Columbus first brought it back from the New World.*

Serves 4 | **Preparation:** 20 minutes | **Cooking and frying time:** 40 minutes

For the chicken

1 kitchen-ready chicken, about 1–1.5 kg (2 lb 4 oz–3 lb 5 oz)
100 ml (3½ fl oz) olive oil
1 onion, finely diced
2 ripe tomatoes, peeled, seeded and diced
1 bay leaf
125 ml (4 fl oz) semi-dry white wine
250 ml (9 fl oz) chicken stock

For the *picada*

10 g (¼ oz) blanched almonds
3–4 saffron threads
1 tablespoon dark chocolate, grated
1 tablespoon breadcrumbs
1 tablespoon cognac
1 tablespoon flat-leaf (Italian) parsley, chopped
8 large Norway lobsters, scampi or crayfish

Divide the chicken into pieces. Season with salt and pepper. Heat a little olive oil in a casserole dish over high heat, add the chicken pieces and sear.

Add the onion and sauté until translucent, then add the tomatoes, bay leaf, white wine and stock. Bring to the boil and simmer everything for 10–15 minutes.

Combine the remaining olive oil and all of the ingredients for the *picada*, except the seafood, in a mortar and pestle and pound to a paste. Add the paste to the chicken, stir in well and return everything to the boil.

Add the Norway lobsters and simmer in the stock for 5–8 minutes. Season with salt and pepper and serve in the casserole dish.

ANEC AL FORN AMB PRUNES I PINYONS

PATO AL HORNO CON CIRUELAS Y PIÑONES | ROAST DUCK WITH PRUNES AND PINE NUTS

People in the region around Barcelona eat a lot of duck, and the nearby Penedès region produces excellent birds. Duck dishes such as this one, which is prepared with prunes, pine nuts and cinnamon, are available year round, even though the ingredients might suggest a Christmas dish.

Serves 4 | **Preparation:** 25 minutes | **Cooking time:** 1 hour 50 minutes

1 kitchen-ready duck, about 1.5 kg (3 lb 5 oz)
1 tablespoon olive oil
2–3 garlic cloves, unpeeled
1 onion, diced
1 carrot, diced
1 small leek, sliced
1 bay leaf
1 sprig thyme
1 cinnamon stick
100 ml (3½ fl oz) white wine
100 ml (3½ fl oz) cognac
2 tomatoes, peeled, seeded and diced
12 prunes, pitted
40 g (1½ oz) pine nuts

Preheat the oven to 160°C (320°F). Season the duck with salt and freshly ground black pepper. Heat the olive oil and garlic in a roasting pan over high heat and brown the duck all over. Add the onion, carrot, leek, bay leaf, thyme and cinnamon stick. Deglaze with a little water. Cook on the middle rack of the preheated oven, basting occasionally with the meat juices and adding a little more water as required.

After 1 hour, add first the wine, then the cognac and reduce the liquid before adding the diced tomatoes. Cook for another 30 minutes, then remove the duck and vegetables from the pan. Remove the garlic and discard. Pass the vegetables and gravy through a sieve. Return to the roasting dish together with the prunes and pine nuts. Quarter the duck and also return to the pan. Continue to cook for another 10 minutes. Arrange decoratively on a large platter and serve with deep-fried potatoes.

CARGOLS AMB SOBRASSADA

CARACOLES CON SOBRASSADA | SNAILS WITH SOBRASSADA SAUSAGE

This method for cooking snails originally comes from Mallorca.
For the recipe below, the snails are pre-cooked.

Serves 4 | **Preparation:** 15 minutes | **Cooking time:** 1 hour 20 minutes

1 kg (2 lb 4 oz) banded snails
1 bay leaf
2–3 sprigs rosemary
5–6 fennel fronds
Olive oil for frying
1 onion, diced
4 large ripe tomatoes,
  peeled, seeded and diced
3–4 slices serrano ham,
  thinly sliced
100 g (3½ oz) sobrassada
  (Mallorcan spreadable
  sausage) in small pieces
1 garlic clove, crushed
1–2 small dried chillies
  (*guindillas*), crumbled
3–4 sprigs flat-leaf (Italian)
  parsley, chopped
1 small red capsicum
  (pepper), roasted, peeled
  and diced
200 ml (7 fl oz) white wine
1 tablespoon dark
  chocolate, grated

Clean the snails under running water and transfer them to a large pot. Add the bay leaf, rosemary and fennel and pour in enough water to cover. Bring to the boil over medium heat and boil for about 1 hour.

Meanwhile, heat the olive oil in a casserole dish and sauté the onion until translucent. Add the tomatoes and ham and season with salt and freshly ground black pepper. Once the tomatoes have softened, stir in the sobrassada until well combined.

Combine the garlic, chilli and parsley to a paste in a mortar and pestle. Dilute the paste with a little cooking water from the snails and add to the tomato mixture. Stir in the capsicum. Add the snails, wine and chocolate and continue to simmer everything for about 20 minutes. Serve with white bread.

LLOM DE CERDO AMB FIGUES

SOLOMILLO DE CERDO CON HIGOS | PORK LOIN WITH FIGS

In the past, most people in Spain, like most people anywhere, could only afford to have meat dishes on special occasions. Pork loin with figs and Pedro Jiménez sauce is a simple, yet sophisticated, meat dish.

Serves 4 | **Preparation:** 15 minutes | **Cooking, frying and roasting time:** 55 minutes

For the side
1 tablespoon raisins
8 dried figs or pitted
  prunes, halved
Sherry for marinating

For the pork loin
1 kg (2 lb 4 oz) pork loin
Olive oil for frying
125 ml (4 fl oz) sweet sherry
  (e.g. Pedro Jiménez)
1 large onion, quartered
  and thinly sliced
1 tablespoon plain
  (all-purpose) flour
150–200 ml (5–7 fl oz)
  hot chicken stock
Sea salt flakes
3–4 small sprigs thyme

PREPARE THE SIDE DISH
Soak the raisins and dried figs or prunes in the sherry and set aside.

ROAST THE PORK LOIN
Preheat the oven to 150°C (300°F). Trim any skin, tendons or fat off the pork loin. Trim off the ends and use elsewhere. Cut the meat into four even pieces. Heat the olive oil in an ovenproof pan over high heat and sear the pork loin all over. Cover, transfer to the middle rack of the oven and roast until cooked through, about 15–20 minutes.

PREPARE THE SAUCE
Deglaze the meat juices in the roasting pan with 125 ml (4 fl oz) sherry. Heat some more olive oil in another pan over medium heat and caramelise the onion with a little salt. Once the onion is lightly caramelised, stir in the flour and cook for another minute before adding the sherry stock. Bring everything to the boil. Add the soaked dried fruit and simmer to reduce somewhat. Pour in the chicken stock and simmer for about 15 minutes to make a creamy gravy. Season with salt and freshly ground black pepper.

PUT THE DISH TOGETHER
Season the pork loin with pepper and arrange the slices on warmed plates. Pour the gravy around the meat slices and divide the dried fruit among the plates. Garnish with sea salt flakes and sprigs of thyme. Serve with potatoes.

PEUS DE PORC AMB BOLETS

PIES DE CERDO CON SETAS | MUSHROOM-STUFFED PIG'S TROTTERS

Once upon a time, literally every single bit of a butchered pig was used in one way or another. Nothing was thrown away, and even the bristles, snout and all offal were put to some use, as were the trotters, which are surprisingly delicious. Catalans have a range of recipes for this somewhat undervalued piece of pork.

Serves 8 | **Preparation:** 40 minutes | **Cooking time:** 2 hours 10 minutes

For the pig's trotters
8 pig's trotters (available
  from butchers)
1 onion, chopped
1 bay leaf
1 clove
5 black peppercorns
1 bunch of soup vegetables,
  cut into large pieces
Olive oil for frying

For the sauce and filling
Olive oil for frying
1 onion, diced
150 ml (5 fl oz) cava
2 tomatoes, peeled,
  seeded and diced
1 kg (2 lb 4 oz) wild
  mushrooms, cleaned
  and diced
1 tablespoon plain
  (all-purpose) flour
12 blanched almonds,
  chopped
12 hazelnuts, chopped
1 tablespoon flat-leaf
  (Italian) parsley leaves
1 garlic clove

COOK THE PIG'S TROTTERS
Thoroughly wash the pig's trotters. Bring to the boil in a pot with plenty of water, together with the onion, bay leaf, clove, peppercorns, soup vegetables and some salt. Simmer for 1½–2 hours. Remove the meat from the stock, leave to cool and carefully remove the bones. Season the meat and sear in a pan with a little added olive oil. Set aside. Strain the stock and reserve.

PREPARE THE SAUCE AND FILLING
Heat some olive oil in a saucepan over low heat and sauté the diced onion. Once the onion starts to colour, gradually deglaze with the cava. Simmer to reduce the liquid and soften the onion. Add the tomatoes and simmer until soft. Season the sauce with salt.

Dust the mushrooms with a little flour. Heat some olive oil in a pan over high heat and sear the mushrooms. Stuff the pig's trotters with the mushrooms, transfer to the pan and drizzle with the sauce. Add a little of the reserved strained stock and simmer everything for 10 minutes over low heat.

Thoroughly pound the nuts, parsley and garlic in a mortar and pestle and sprinkle over the dish. Simmer for another 10 minutes, season with salt and pepper and serve.

SECRETO IBÉRICO

SECRETO IBÉRICO | 'HIDDEN' FILLET

Secreto ibérico or presa ibérica *is a delicacy that may not be very readily available, but is invariably greeted with great enthusiasm whenever it is. This cut of pork is a fan-shaped muscle located between a pig's saddle and loin. Depending on how the pork is cut, this section of loin is often hardly discernible between the layers of fat, hence the name 'hidden' fillet. It is richly marbled with fat, giving it its unique flavour.*

Serves 4 | **Preparation:** 10 minutes | **Resting time:** 12 hours | **Cooking time:** 10 minutes

4 *secretos* or 2 fan-shaped
   secreto pieces
A little olive oil
Herbs to taste, e.g.
   rosemary or thyme
1 garlic clove, thinly sliced
Sea salt flakes

PREPARATION

Marinate the *secreto ibérico* overnight in the olive oil, herbs and garlic.

Grill (broil) the marinated meat over high heat until medium done. Slice into fine strips. Sprinkle with sea salt flakes and enjoy. This matches perfectly with *pimientos de padrón* (see page 34) or any other fried vegetables or deep-fried potatoes.

TIP

The best *secreto* fillets come from year-old, pure-bred Iberian pigs that are kept half wild on dehesa agro-forestry land and fed on *belloras* (acorns) for three months.

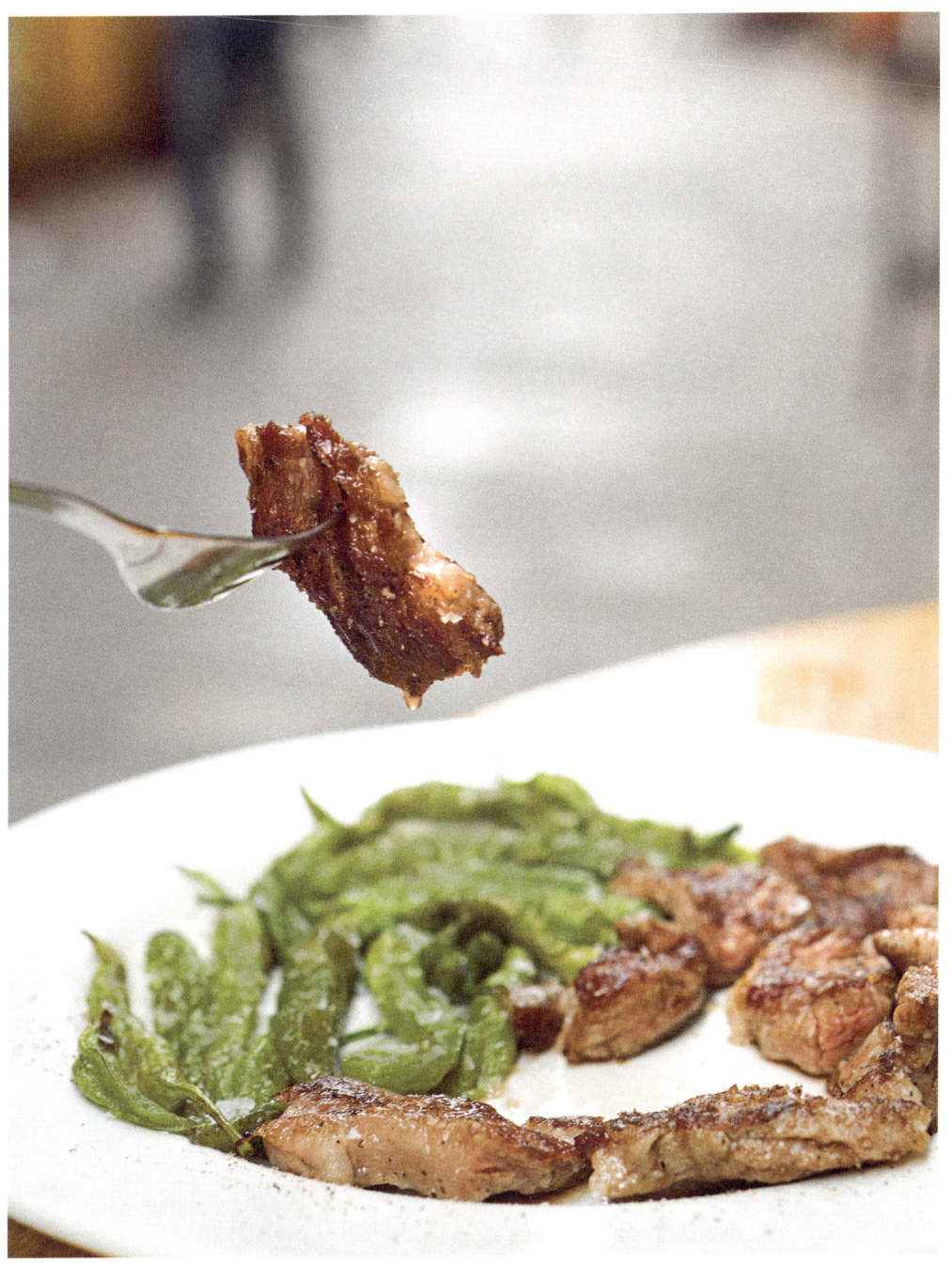

CONILL AMB CARGOLS O NÍSCALOS

CONEJO CON CARACOLES O ROVELLONS | RABBIT WITH SNAILS OR RED PINE MUSHROOMS

Catalan mushroom dishes, which are often cooked according to old family recipes, are as varied as they are tasty. The recipe below combines mushrooms with rabbit, cooked in a rich sauce, to create an incredibly aromatic delight.

Serves 4 | **Preparation:** 35 minutes | **Cooking and frying time:** 1¼ hours

1 rabbit, divided into pieces
1 tablespoon plain
    (all-purpose) flour
Olive oil for frying
1 carrot, diced
1 large onion, diced
1 green capsicum
    (pepper), diced
1 small ripe tomato, peeled,
    seeded and diced
2 garlic cloves, unpeeled
125 ml (4 fl oz) red wine
1 teaspoon dried marjoram
1 tablespoon basil, chopped
1 tablespoon flat-leaf
    (Italian) parsley, chopped
1 rabbit liver
4 hazelnuts
4 almonds
500 g (1 lb 2 oz) snails
Vinegar
Mixed fresh herbs

Season the rabbit meat with salt and freshly ground black pepper and dust with flour. Sear all over in olive oil in a large casserole dish over high heat. Add the carrot, onion, capsicum, tomato and garlic. Braise everything for about 30–40 minutes, turning the meat occasionally. Once the rabbit is golden brown all over, deglaze with the red wine. Add water, little by little, if the pan dries out. Sprinkle with the herbs.

Heat a little olive oil in a small frying pan over medium heat and fry the rabbit liver for 5 minutes. Crush the liver together with the hazelnuts and almonds in a mortar and pestle and stir the resulting paste in with the rabbit in the casserole dish. Continue to braise for 5–10 minutes until the meat is cooked through and tender. Remove the rabbit from the sauce and keep warm. Remove the garlic cloves. Blend the sauce with a stick blender and pass through a sieve. Return the sauce to the casserole dish.

Wash the snails in water with some added salt and vinegar, then rinse them well under running water. Transfer the snails and mixed herbs to a pot of cold water. Heat slowly and simmer for about 30 minutes. Drain and add to the rabbit in the casserole dish. Briefly return everything to the boil and serve.

This is absolutely delicious with simple boiled potatoes.

TIP
Alternatively, heat some olive oil in a frying pan over high heat and sear red pine mushrooms briefly. Season with salt and pepper and add to the sauce together with all of the mushroom juices. Simmer in the sauce for about 10 minutes over medium heat until cooked through. Transfer the rabbit onto a warmed platter, drizzle with the sauce and arrange the mushrooms around the rabbit. Serve immediately.

CIVET DE SENGLAR

CIVET DE JABALÍ | BRAISED WILD BOAR

In autumn and winter, many restaurants in Barcelona serve a whole range of so-called civet *dishes. This way of preparing meat goes back to the Middle Ages: it involves marinating the meat in wine, blood and lots of onions for at least 24 hours before it is braised. The* picada *is a particularly important part of this recipe.*

Serves 6 | **Preparation:** 30 minutes | **Frying and cooking time:** 2 hours 40 minutes
Marinating time: 2 days

For the meat and gravy

1.5 kg (3 lb 5 oz) wild
    boar meat
1–2 bottles red wine
2 large onions, coarsely
    chopped
2 carrots, coarsely chopped
1 stick celery with leaves
1 garlic clove, thinly sliced
2 bay leaves
1 clove
2 sprigs thyme
12 black peppercorns
Olive oil for frying
150 g (5½ oz) bacon, diced
2 tablespoons plain
    (all-purpose) flour
1 small glass cognac
Meat stock

For the *picada*

1 slice stale baguette
4–5 sprigs flat-leaf
    (Italian) parsley
1 small garlic clove, finely diced
5 almonds, chopped
5 hazelnuts, chopped
1 tablespoon pine nuts
1 tablespoon grated dark
    chocolate

PREPARE AND BRAISE THE MEAT

Dice the meat and season with salt and pepper. Pour the red wine over the meat, vegetables, garlic and spices in a large bowl, ensuring that everything is well covered. Cover the bowl and set aside in the refrigerator to marinate for 24–48 hours. Stir and turn occasionally. Remove the meat and vegetables from the marinade, drain and set aside. Bring the marinade to the boil over high heat and reduce to a quarter of its volume.

Heat a large saucepan over medium heat, add the olive oil and fry the bacon until golden brown. Remove from the saucepan and set aside.

Dust the meat with flour and sear in olive oil over high heat. Deglaze with the cognac. Dice the onion and carrots from the marinade, add to the meat in the pan and continue to fry. Pass the marinade through a sieve and add to the meat. If necessary, add some extra stock to cover the meat.

Use kitchen twine to tie the bay leaves and thyme sprigs from the marinade to a bouquet together with the celery leaves. Add to the meat along with the fried bacon. Simmer over low heat, stirring occasionally, for 2–2½ hours. Remove the herb bouquet after 2 hours.

PREPARE THE *PICADA*

For the *picada*, dice the baguette and chop the parsley. Pound all ingredients together in a mortar and pestle, then combine with a little of the gravy. Add to the gravy about 10 minutes before the end of the cooking time. Serve in a warmed bowl. This matches perfectly with mashed potatoes or any other type of vegetables.

ARRÒS AMB CONILL

ARROZ CON CONEJO | RABBIT ON RICE

Catalans love eating rabbit, and the best rabbit dishes are made with wild rabbits, of course.
Many restaurants in the countryside cook the rice for this dish with banded snails for extra
flavour and richness; this also makes a very popular, typically Catalan dish.

Serves 4 | **Preparation:** 30 minutes | **Frying and cooking time:** 1 hour

1 rabbit, from a butcher
100 ml (3½ fl oz) olive oil
1 onion, finely diced
3 large ripe tomatoes,
   peeled, seeded and diced
1 garlic clove, unpeeled
1 green capsicum (pepper),
   finely diced
2 artichoke hearts, from a jar
200 g (7 oz) fresh or
   frozen peas
300 g (10½ oz) short-
   grain rice
4–5 sprigs flat-leaf (Italian)
   parsley, leaves picked
4–6 saffron threads

Divide the rabbit and cut the meat into cubes about 2 cm (¾ inch) in size. Heat about half of the olive oil in a casserole dish over high heat. Add the rabbit pieces and sear all over. Season with salt and freshly ground black pepper and remove from the dish. Add the onion, tomatoes, garlic clove and capsicum to the same dish, together with some extra oil if necessary. Sauté over medium heat and reduce a little. Return the rabbit to the dish and deglaze with 1 litre (35 fl oz) water. Simmer for about 20 minutes. Add the artichoke hearts, peas and rice. Continue to cook for another 20 minutes, adding more water as needed.

Meanwhile, pound the parsley leaves and saffron threads with the remaining olive oil. Stir the mixture into the meat and rice 5 minutes before they have finished cooking and season once more with salt and pepper.

ESCUDELLA I CARN D'OLLA

ESCUDELLA I CARN D'OLLA | CATALAN MEAT STEW

To me, escudella *is the most Catalan and most complex stew that I know. Most people only ever cook it for Christmas because of the number of ingredients and the considerable effort required to prepare it. Getting a good* escudella *in a basic restaurant is next to impossible, but a few good restaurants offer this stew instead of a full three-course menu during the Christmas season. My friend Marc Robles i Montes has found an easier way to prepare* escudella*, though: he had his grandmother sew a number of cotton drawstring bags, which he fills with the various ingredients for the stew and cooks all at once in a large pot. He then only needs to remove the ingredients from the bags to be able to serve them separately. True Catalan ingenuity!*

Serves 6–8 | **Preparation:** 25 minutes | **Cooking time:** 2 hours 40 minutes | **Soaking time:** 12 hours

250 g (9 oz) *gallets*
(large pasta shells)

For the *pilotas*
300 g (10½ oz) mixed
minced (ground) meat
1 garlic clove, crushed
3–4 sprigs flat-leaf (Italian)
parsley, finely chopped
150 g (5½ oz) air-dried meat,
finely chopped
1 egg
1 small stale bread roll,
soaked in milk and excess
milk squeezed out
1 pinch ground cinnamon

Continued opposite

PREPARE THE *PILOTA* MIXTURE

Mix the minced meat, garlic, parsley, air-dried meat, egg and soaked bread roll until well combined. Season with salt, freshly ground black pepper and cinnamon and refrigerate.

COOK THE *ESCUDELLA*

Place all of the meat, except for the sausages, and the bones in a very large pot together with 5 litres (175 fl oz) water and the legumes. Bring to the boil. Add salt, cover and simmer for about 1 hour over medium heat. Skim off any foam regularly. Meanwhile, wash, trim and coarsely chop the vegetables. Quarter the cabbage. Add everything to the pot with the meat, except for the potatoes, cabbage and sausages. Cover again and continue to cook for another 45 minutes.

Shape the *pilota* into a loaf. Add to the pot together with the potatoes and simmer everything for another 20 minutes. Add the cabbage and simmer for 10 more minutes. Finally add the sausages and simmer gently for a final 5 minutes. Season with salt.

PUT THE STEW TOGETHER

Remove some stock from the pot and use it to cook the pasta until al dente. Keep the meat and vegetables warm in the remaining stock. Slice the meat and *pilota* and serve on a warmed platter together with the sausages, vegetables and legumes.

For the *escudella*

500 g (1 lb 2 oz) beef
200 g (7 oz) pig's snout
  and/or pig's ears
  (from a butcher)
½ pig's trotter
1 large veal bone
  (from a butcher)
½ kitchen-ready chicken
100 g (3½ oz) air-dried meat
200 g (7 oz) dried cannellini
  beans, soaked overnight
200 g (7 oz) dried chickpeas,
  soaked overnight
2 carrots
1 small turnip
½ leek
1 onion
1 stick celery
1 parsnip
8 waxy potatoes
1 small white cabbage
1 each butifarra blanca
  and negra (not blood
  pudding!), skins pricked

CANELONS D'ESTIL CATALÀ

CANELONES AL ESTILO CATALÁN | CATALAN CANNELLONI

The first written record of canelones *apparently goes back to 1815, and they have been a staple of Catalan cooking since then. Cannelloni has been among the traditional dishes to be served at Catalan Christmas dinners for generations.*

Serves 6 | **Preparation:** 35 minutes | **Frying, cooking and baking time:** 50 minutes

For the filling

Olive oil for frying
1 skinless chicken breast
  fillet, diced
200 g (7 oz) chicken
  liver, diced
500 g (1 lb 2 oz) lean mixed
  minced (ground) meat
1 large onion, diced
1 small leek, sliced
1 garlic clove, crushed
1 bay leaf
3 ripe tomatoes, peeled,
  seeded and diced
100 ml (3½ fl oz) dessert
  wine
2 tablespoons breadcrumbs

Continued opposite

PREPARE THE FILLING

Heat some olive oil in a large, deep frying pan over high heat and fry the chicken fillet, liver, minced meat, onion, leek, garlic and bay leaf until everything starts to colour. Add the diced tomatoes and reduce the liquid. Add the wine, cover and simmer everything for 15 minutes over low heat.

Remove the pan from the heat and stir in the breadcrumbs if the mixture seems too thin. Season with salt and freshly ground black pepper.

PREPARE THE *CANELONES*

Pre-cook the pasta sheets in boiling water with a dash of olive oil according to the packet instructions. Refresh under cold water and lay the sheets out on a clean tea towel.

PREPARE THE BÉCHAMEL SAUCE

Melt the butter in a saucepan over medium heat. Stir in the flour and sweat. Add the stock and milk, stirring constantly, and bring everything to the boil. Reduce the heat and simmer for 10 minutes. Season with thyme, parsley, nutmeg, salt and pepper.

PUT TOGETHER THE *CANELONES*

Preheat the oven to 180°C (350°F). Place 1½ tablespoons of the filling on each pasta sheet. Roll up the sheets around the filling and transfer them to a greased ovenproof dish. Cover with the béchamel sauce and sprinkle with cheese. Dot with shaved butter and bake on the middle rack of the oven for about 15 minutes or until golden on top.

For the *canelones* and the béchamel sauce

24 pasta sheets

Olive oil for cooking

50 g (1¾ oz) butter, plus some extra shavings

60 g (2¼ oz) plain (all-purpose) flour

500 ml (17 fl oz) chicken stock

500 ml (17 fl oz) milk

1 pinch ground thyme

1 teaspoon dried parsley

1 pinch freshly grated nutmeg

100 g (3½ oz) grated cheese (e.g. emmental)

The view from the Basílica de Santa Maria del Mar onto the narrow lanes of the Born/La Ribera quarter.

Oh, and Barcelona's to-die-for desserts... Most Catalan desserts are incredibly sweet and immensely rich. For some, they are heaven on a plate, while others think of them more as instruments of culinary torture.

Most of these recipes would be a long way outside any dietary guidelines, but they also include some that are not quite as rich and will delight people like me, who aren't too fond of overly sweet foods.

DESSERTS

CREMA CATALANA

CREMA CATALANA | CREMA CATALANA

One of the best-known Spanish temptations must surely be crema catalana, *a dessert that has been prepared mainly (but by no means only) for San José's Day on 19 March for centuries. It is also known under the name of crème brûlée, because a certain Frenchman casually forgot to mention where he had first enjoyed this dessert when he included it in his cookbook about a century ago. Originally, the delightfully crunchy layer on top was caramelised with a specially made iron, heated to red-hot over an open fire and then passed over the sugary cream. An easier way is to use the oven grill (broiler) or, even quicker, a small kitchen blowtorch.*

Serves 4 | **Preparation:** 10 minutes | **Cooking time:** 10 minutes | **Chilling time:** 5 hours

200 g (7 oz) sugar
4 egg yolks
1 tablespoon cornflour (cornstarch)
Grated zest of ½ organic lemon or orange
1 cinnamon stick
500 ml (17 fl oz) milk

Place 150 g (5½ oz) of the sugar and the egg yolks in a saucepan and whisk until foamy. Add the cornflour, lemon zest and cinnamon stick and stir in the milk. Gradually heat the mixture over medium heat, stirring constantly, until the cream begins to set.

Remove the cinnamon stick and divide the cream among four heatproof ramekins. Leave to cool and then refrigerate for 4–5 hours. Before serving, sprinkle the remaining sugar on top of the cream and melt it until golden brown, using a kitchen blowtorch or oven grill (broiler). Serve immediately.

In Barcelona, *crema catalana* is often served with filleted orange segments.

FLAN

FLAN DE HUEVOS | EGG CUSTARD

*Flan would be one of the best-known and most popular desserts
in all of Spain, both in restaurants and in home cooking.*

Serves 6 | Preparation: 15 minutes | **Cooking time:** 50 minutes
Resting time: 30 minutes | **Chilling time:** 4 hours

300 g (10½ oz) sugar
1 teaspoon lemon juice
500 ml (17 fl oz) milk
1 vanilla pod
4 large eggs
2 egg yolks

Add 150 g (5½ oz) of the sugar and 4 tablespoons water to a saucepan
together with the lemon juice and caramelise until golden brown, but
be careful not to burn the mixture. Divide the caramel among six flan
moulds (about 1 tablespoon in each one). Gently shake the moulds to
distribute the caramel evenly.

Slowly heat the milk in another saucepan over medium heat.
Scrape the seeds out of the vanilla pod and add both the seeds and
pod to the milk. Take the mixture off the heat just before it starts
to boil. Cover and leave to rest for 30 minutes.

Preheat the oven to 160°C (320°F); do not use the fan-forced
setting. Combine the eggs, egg yolks and remaining 150 g (5½ oz)
of the sugar in a bowl and whisk until lightly foamy. Stir in the
cooled milk mixture, discarding the vanilla pod. Carefully pour the
cream into the moulds. Place the moulds inside a larger baking dish
and pour enough hot water into the dish to come up halfway. Bake
until set, about 40 minutes. Remove from the oven as soon as the
cream has set. Leave to cool to room temperature. Cover the moulds
with plastic wrap and refrigerate for at least 4 hours before serving.

To serve, carefully separate the flans from the moulds using
a sharp knife and invert onto small plates.

MEL I MATÓ

MEL I MATÓ | CREAM CHEESE WITH HONEY

Mató is a delicate, unsalted yet mildly savoury goat's cream cheese from the Catalan Pyrenées. It is used to make the classic Spanish dessert mel i mató, that is, cream cheese with honey. Because mató is not very readily available in Australia, I have provided a recipe with slightly modified ingredients below.

Serves 4 | **Preparation:** 10 minutes | **Cooking time:** 10 minutes | **Chilling time:** 6 hours

2 litres (70 fl oz) milk
Zest of 1 organic lemon, peeled off in a single, broad strip
20 g (¾ oz) rennet (available from specialist suppliers) or vinegar
Honey
Walnut kernels
Pine nuts or fresh seasonal fruit

Place the milk in a saucepan together with the lemon zest and simmer for 10 minutes, then leave to cool to 70°C (160°F). Dissolve the rennet in a little water and gradually add 4 tablespoons of this mixture (or the vinegar) to the milk until it coagulates. Remove the lemon zest and leave the mixture to cool for 4–5 hours.

Drain any liquid whey, if desired, or leave it in with the cream cheese, depending on the preferred consistency. Transfer the cream cheese to a sieve and leave it to drain well, then divide it among four small moulds and refrigerate until the cheese has set and firmed up.

To serve, invert the moulds onto plates, drizzle with honey and garnish with the walnuts, pine nuts and/or fresh fruit.

TORRADETES DE SANTA TERESA

TORRIJAS CON VINO | DRUNKEN FRENCH TOASTS

This traditional dessert is quite similar to French toast. In Barcelona, it is mainly served during semana santa, the Holy Week before Easter.

Serves 4 | **Preparation:** 15 minutes | **Cooking and frying time:** 25 minutes

1 litre (35 fl oz) milk
1 vanilla pod
2 cinnamon sticks
250 g (9 oz) sugar
Zest of ½ organic lemon, peeled off in a single strip
100 ml (3½ fl oz) wine, plus some extra for drizzling
3 eggs
Olive oil for frying
1 small loaf of stale white bread, thickly sliced
Cinnamon sugar

Place the milk into a saucepan. Scrape the seeds out of the vanilla pod and add both the seeds and pod to the milk along with the cinnamon sticks, sugar and lemon zest. Bring to the boil. Take the saucepan off the heat and leave to cool to room temperature. Strain the mixture into a bowl. Stir in the wine. Whisk the eggs until foamy in a separate bowl.

Heat the olive oil in a large pan over medium heat. Dip the bread slices into the milk mixture and drag them through the whisked eggs. Transfer to the pan and fry them in the olive oil for 2–3 minutes each side. Remove from the pan, drain excess oil on paper towel and sprinkle with cinnamon sugar. Drizzle with a little wine just before serving.

POMA AL FORN

MANZANA ASADA EN HOJALDRE | BAKED APPLES IN PUFF PASTRY

*Baked apples have been widely enjoyed in Spain for ages. These baked apples
in puff pastry with blackcurrant sauce are a popular dessert for autumn and winter.
They are very easy to prepare and taste amazing.*

Serves 4 | **Preparation:** 20 minutes | **Cooking and baking time:** 20 minutes

For the apples

30 g (1 oz) butter, softened
60 g (2¼ oz) sugar, plus
  some extra for the pastry
80 g (2¾ oz) blanched
  almonds, chopped
1 tablespoon raisins
½ teaspoon ground
  cinnamon
4 apples
400 g (14 oz) puff pastry

For the blackcurrant sauce

30 g (1 oz) sugar
3 tablespoons blackcurrant
  jam
1 tablespoon cornflour
  (cornstarch)
1 teaspoon lemon juice
1 tablespoon blackcurrants

BAKE THE APPLES

Preheat the oven to 180°C (350°F). Combine the butter, sugar,
almonds, raisins and cinnamon in a bowl. Peel the apples and
remove the cores. Fill them with the nut and raisin mixture.

Roll out the puff pastry and cut it into strips about 2 cm
(¾ inch) wide. Pour the sugar into a flat dish and roll the apples
in it. Wrap the apples with slightly overlapping strips of puff pastry,
starting from the bottom and leaving a gap at the top. Transfer
the apples to an ovenproof dish and bake them on the middle rack
of the oven for about 20 minutes until the puff pastry has turned
golden brown.

PREPARE THE BLACKCURRANT SAUCE

Meanwhile, put the sugar and jam in a saucepan together with 100 ml
(3½ fl oz) water. Heat slowly, stirring, over medium heat. Dissolve the
cornflour in 50 ml (1½ fl oz) cold water and add to the jam mixture
once it has come to the boil. Reduce the temperature and simmer for
5 more minutes. Stir in the lemon juice. Add the blackcurrants to the
sauce and heat through for 2 minutes.

Serve the hot baked apples together with the sauce.

PANELLETS

PANELLETS | MARZIPAN CONFECTIONERY

In Catalan-speaking regions, this sweet is traditionally made for All Saint's Day on 1 November. As rich as it is, it would also make a truly indulgent Christmas treat.

Makes about 25 large or 40–50 small balls | **Preparation:** 30 minutes
Resting time: 3 hours | **Baking time:** 10 minutes

250 g (9 oz) sugar
Grated zest of 1 organic
   lemon
250 g (9 oz) ground
   almonds
125 g (4½ oz) potatoes,
   boiled and peeled
1 egg
70 g (2½ oz) desiccated
   coconut
70 g (2½ oz) pine nuts
50 g (1¾ oz) whole,
   blanched almonds

Combine the sugar, lemon zest and ground almonds in a bowl. Mash the potatoes with a fork. Separate the egg and set the egg white aside. Combine the potatoes with three-quarters of the egg yolk and set the remaining egg yolk aside. Add the potatoes to the sugar mixture. Use an electric mixer or food processor to form a dough, mixing for at least 1 minute. If the dough is still too soft, add some more ground almonds; if it is too dry, add the remaining egg yolk. Refrigerate for 2–3 hours.

Combine half the dough with 50 g (1¾ oz) desiccated coconut. Roll out on baking paper, cut into pieces about 3 cm (1¼ inches) square and shape these into balls. Roll the coconut *panellets* in the left-over coconut and place them on a baking tray lined with baking paper.

Prepare the remaining half of the dough following the same method, but using pine nuts. Brush the balls with egg white, roll them in the remaining pine nuts and place them on the baking tray. Press whole almonds on top of the *panellets*.

Preheat the oven grill (broiler) to 130°C (250°F). Bake the *panellets* on the middle rack of the oven until lightly browned, about 10 minutes.

Panellets, like all marzipan confectionery, dry out quickly and should therefore be stored in an airtight container and consumed soon after baking.

LA VIDA ES DULCE

As all Spaniards, the Catalans like it sweet, perhaps because life is sweet in Catalonia. At least that's the impression given by the incredible abundance of pastry and chocolate shops in Barcelona. It's a real challenge to choose just a few of the most tempting of these shops, and the ones mentioned in this book shall stand for the entire trade and its rich local tradition.

Quite a few people are a little wary of visiting the 'Bubó' chocolaterie because they know only too well that, once they have stepped across its threshold, it won't be easy to leave again, at least not without some indulgent purchases. Another favourite source of sweet temptations is the 'Cacao Sampaka', which served hot chocolate with chilli long before the movie 'Chocolat' graced our screens. 'Caelum, delicias y otras tentaciones de Monasterio' – the name of this Barcelona café says it all: 'heaven, delicacies and other temptations from the monastery'. All of the delicacies it sells are prepared by nuns and monks.

And Barcelona's many, many classic bakeries tempt visitors with a huge range of sweet pastries made using traditional recipes that are definitely not aimed at the diet-conscious.

COCA DE SANT JOAN

COCA DE SAN JUAN | ST JOHN'S CAKE

Coca de Sant Joan *is one of the most popular cakes in Barcelona and its surroundings. Traditionally, it is served on the eve of St John's Day, on the night from 23 to 24 June. There are thousands of variations — with or without candied fruit, with a cream made of egg yolks, sugar, milk and vanilla, with sugar and pine nuts, even with diced bacon… Decide for yourself which you like best.*

Makes 1 cake | **Preparation:** 20 minutes | **Rising time:** 45 minutes | **Baking time:** 20 minutes

For the St John's cake
25 g (1 oz) yeast
100 ml (3½ fl oz) lukewarm
  milk
250 g (9 oz) plain
  (all-purpose) flour
100 g (3½ oz) sugar
100 g (3½ oz) butter
2 eggs
1 pinch salt
½ teaspoon ground aniseed
½ teaspoon ground
  cinnamon
Grated zest of ½ an
  organic lemon
Oil or butter for the
  baking tray

For the garnish
1 egg, whisked
Candied fruit
Pine nuts
Sugar

Dissolve the yeast in the milk in a small bowl. Stir in 3 tablespoons of the flour to make a starter. Cover and leave the mixture to rest in a warm place for about 15 minutes.

Once the yeast mixture has doubled in volume, add the remaining cake ingredients and work them together to form a smooth dough. Cover again and leave to rest in a warm place for about 15 minutes until the volume has doubled again.

Shape the mixture into an oval about 1 cm (½ inch) thick and transfer to a greased baking tray. Brush with the whisked egg and decorate with the candied fruits. Leave to rest again for about 15 minutes until the volume has doubled once more. Meanwhile, preheat the oven to 160°C (320°F). Sprinkle the cake with pine nuts and sugar and bake on the middle rack of the oven for 20 minutes.

BRAÇ DE GITANO CON CREMA QUEMADA

BRAZO DE GITANO CON CREMA QUEMADA | GYPSY'S ARM CAKE

In Barcelona, when you invite guests to your home for dinner, they often bring dessert, and one of the most popular sweets to bring along is brazo de gitano. *In Australia, where we have become very politically correct, this pastry would have long been removed from any official record, as its name literally means 'gypsy's arm'.*

Makes 1 cake | **Preparation:** 35 minutes | **Cooking and baking time:** 25 minutes

For the filling
1 litre (35 fl oz) milk
Zest of 1 organic lemon,
 peeled off in a single strip
1 cinnamon stick
1 teaspoon vanilla sugar
200 g (7 oz) icing
 (confectioners') sugar
70 g (2½ oz) cornflour
 (cornstarch)
6 egg yolks
20 g (¾ oz) butter
Sugar for sprinkling

For the sponge cake
3 egg whites
1 pinch salt
75 g (2½ oz) sugar
2 teaspoons vanilla sugar
3 egg yolks
75 g (2½ oz) plain
 (all-purpose) flour
3 teaspoons baking powder

PREPARE THE FILLING

Bring 750 ml (26 fl oz) of the milk, the lemon zest, cinnamon stick and vanilla sugar to the boil in a saucepan, stirring. Take off the heat and leave to cool a little.

Pour the remaining milk into a tall bowl and whisk in first the icing sugar, then the cornflour and finally the egg yolks. Remove and discard the cinnamon stick and lemon zest from the cooled milk and stir in the egg yolk mixture. Transfer to a double boiler and heat over low heat, stirring constantly, until it starts to set. As soon as the cream reaches a uniform consistency, take it off the heat and whisk in the butter. Leave to cool.

BAKE THE SPONGE MIXTURE AND SHAPE INTO A ROLL

Preheat the oven to 160°C (320°F). Beat the egg whites, salt, half of the sugar and the vanilla sugar until stiff.

Whisk the egg yolks and the remaining sugar until foamy in another bowl. Very carefully fold the beaten egg whites into the egg yolk mixture. Sift the flour and baking powder on top and fold in carefully.

Spread the sponge mixture evenly on a Swiss roll tin lined with baking paper and bake for 10 minutes. Remove from the oven and transfer the sponge to a clean tea towel. Trim the edges with a knife to straighten. Roll up the sponge using the towel and leave to cool.

Once cool, carefully unroll the sponge again and spread it evenly with three-quarters of the filling, about 5 mm (¼ inch) thick. Leave the last 3–5 cm (1¼–2 inches) of the sponge uncovered. Roll the sponge up again, starting from the side with the filling all the way to the edge. Use the remaining filling to seal both ends of the roll and spread it all over the outside. Sprinkle the cake with plenty of sugar. Caramelise the sugar with a small kitchen blowtorch, as you would with a *crema catalana*.

FIGUES AMB FORMATGE DE CABRA

COLL DE DAMA CON QUESO DE CABRA ⎪ GOAT'S CHEESE IN A RICE PAPER PARCEL

Personally, I don't often have desserts in restaurants, simply because I'm too full already or what's on offer is too sweet for my taste. Nevertheless, some chefs have been able to entice me to have dessert, mostly when their recipes involve a clever combination of sweet and savoury flavours, as is often the case in Spain. By the way: the best figs you can get anywhere in Catalonia are deliciously named Coll de dama, or 'Lady's neck'.

Serves 4 ⎪ **Preparation:** 15 minutes ⎪ **Cooking time:** 5 minutes

4 figs (use Coll de dama,
  if available)
4 small sprigs rosemary
4 small round goat's cheese
  (e.g. Cabécou)
4 rice paper sheets, soaked
  in water
Olive oil for frying
A little balsamic vinegar

Remove the stem bases from the figs and cut a slice 1 cm (½ inch) thick out of the thickest section of each fig. Finely dice the remaining fruit. Trim the soft tips off the rosemary sprigs and set aside. Pick off some leaves from the remaining sprigs, chop and combine with the diced figs in a bowl.

Stack 1 rosemary tip, 1 slice of fig and 1 goat's cheese round in the centre of each sheet of softened rice paper. Fold the rice paper in to make a small parcel.

Heat plenty of olive oil in a pan over high heat and fry the parcels, seam side down, for 2–3 minutes until golden brown, then flip over and cook the other side for another 2 minutes.

Season the diced fig and rosemary mixture to taste with balsamic vinegar and serve it with the golden brown cheese parcels.

SORBET DE PRUNES

SORBETE DE CIRUELA | PLUM SORBET

Spain is blessed with an abundance of vegetable- and fruit-growing areas. The fertile Ebro valley produces an excellent variety of plums, among others. In Barcelona, these are often transformed into a beautifully coloured, refreshing sorbet.

Serves 4 | **Preparation:** 10 minutes | **Cooking time:** 20 minutes | **Freezing time:** 5 hours

7–9 large, ripe plums
3 tablespoons sugar
1 cinnamon stick, plus extra
   for garnish
1 star anise, plus extra
   for garnish
200 ml (7 fl oz) red wine

Halve the plums and remove the stones. Quarter one plum and set aside.

Heat the sugar with 3 tablespoons water in a saucepan over medium heat. As soon as the sugar starts to brown, add the plum halves and stir well to prevent the sugar from burning. Add the large cinnamon stick and the star anise. Simmer for 4–5 minutes, then deglaze with the wine and continue to simmer until the plums are soft.

Remove the cinnamon stick and star anise. Strain the fruit purée through a sieve and sweeten to taste. Leave the mixture to cool, then transfer to an ice cream maker to churn; alternatively, freeze for a few hours in a bowl. If freezing, stir the mixture regularly, every 30 minutes if possible, to break down any ice crystals as they form.

Serve the sorbet in chilled cocktail glasses, garnished with a plum wedge, cinnamon sticks and star anise.

This sorbet also tastes great with doughnut peaches or any other sweet, aromatic fruit of your choice.

TARONJA, TARONJA I TARONJA

NARANJA, NARANJA Y NARANJA | ORANGES THREE WAYS

Oranges are fantastic fruits. Both the delicious, healthy pulp and the highly aromatic zest (without any of the white skin) are perfect for using in the kitchen. There's plenty of scope for pleasant surprises.

Serves 4 | **Preparation:** 20 minutes | **Cooking time:** 1 hour 5 minutes | **Marinating time:** 3 hours

8 organic oranges
2–3 tablespoons sugar
50 ml (1½ fl oz) orange
    liqueur (Grand Marnier
    or Cointreau)

Peel the zest from the oranges, keeping the strips not too short, but making them as thin as possible. Be careful to avoid any of the white skin, as it is bitter. Slice the orange zest into thin julienne strips. Add the orange zest to a saucepan of boiling water and simmer for 15–20 minutes. Strain and set aside.

Dissolve the sugar in 4 tablespoons water in a small saucepan over low heat, then add the orange zest. Simmer for 45 minutes or until all of the liquid has evaporated and the sugar starts to crystallise. Be careful not to let the sugar brown. Transfer the orange zest strips to a sheet of foil, ideally keeping the strips separate so they do not stick together. Leave to cool.

Fillet the oranges, reserving any juice. Transfer the orange fillets to a bowl and cover with the liqueur. Marinate in the refrigerator for 3 hours. Refrigerate the reserved orange juice as well.

To serve, divide the orange fillets among four glass bowls. Drizzle with the marinade and juice and garnish with the candied orange peel.

'El Xampanyet' in Barcelona's Carrer de Montcada likes to serve *xampán* al fresco in classic champagne saucers.

NÍSPEROS EN ORUJO

NÍSPEROS EN ORUJO | MEDLAR WITH ORUJO SPIRIT

Medlars are an incredibly healthy fruit that are also excellent for preserving. Preserved medlars form the basis for this delicious dessert served in Barcelona's 'Quimet & Quimet', a tapas bar steeped in Catalan tradition. Orujo is a spirit distilled from grape marc. It is similar to grappa, but higher in alcohol. Orujo is usually consumed chilled. This dessert is as simple as it is unconventional.

Serves 4 | **Preparation:** 5 minutes

4 medlars from a jar
  (available from specialist
  suppliers)
Orujo (grape marc spirit)
Medlar syrup (from the jar)
Ground cinnamon

Quarter the medlars and transfer the quarters to large shot glasses or cocktail glasses. Fill the glasses one-third with *orujo* and two-thirds with medlar syrup.

Pierce the medlar pieces a few times and dust them with cinnamon. Serve with a fork and spoon – done!

SORBET DE MANDARINA

SORBETE DE MANDARINA | MANDARIN SORBET

Spanish sweets and desserts are (in)famous for being just that: sweet. But there are some exceptions that are less sweet and all the more refreshing, among them this sorbet.

Serves 4 | **Preparation:** 10 minutes | **Marinating time:** 1 hour | **Chilling time:** 5 hours

2–3 cm (¾–1¼ inch) piece fresh ginger
Juice of 8 sweet, aromatic organic mandarins
40 ml (1¼ fl oz) vodka
1 pinch ground allspice
2 mandarin slices, halved
4 sprigs mint

Peel and mince the ginger. Combine with the mandarin juice in a bowl. Stir in the vodka and season with allspice.

Leave the mixture to marinate in the refrigerator for 1 hour. Strain and transfer to an ice cream maker to churn; alternatively, freeze for 4–5 hours in a bowl. If freezing, keep stirring the mixture regularly, every 30 minutes if possible, to break down any ice crystals as they form.

Serve the sorbet in chilled cocktail glasses, garnished with half a mandarin slice and a sprig of mint each.

SORBET DE SINDRÍA AMB ALFABREGA

SORBETE DE SANDÍA CON ALBAHACA | WATERMELON SORBET WITH BASIL

I love dining out, and I love culinary surprises. With some restaurants, I've come to a kind of agreement, where they'll divulge their recipe if I'm able to guess all of the ingredients by taste. It's an intriguing deal for me, through which I've managed to uncover the secrets of this summery dessert.

Serves 4 | **Preparation:** 10 minutes | **Freezing time:** 4 hours

¼ ripe watermelon
80 g (2¾ oz) fresh basil
  leaves, plus some extra
  for garnish
Icing (confectioners') sugar
Rosewater

Dice the watermelon into 2–3 cm (¾–1¼ inch) pieces. Reserve any juice and remove as many of the seeds as possible. Transfer the pieces to a bowl and freeze for 3–4 hours. Refrigerate the reserved juice.

Just before serving, sprinkle the basil leaves with plenty of icing sugar and chop very finely to make a coarse paste that shouldn't be too firm.

Quickly blend the frozen watermelon and chilled watermelon juice to a sorbet in a blender or food processor.

Divide the sorbet among chilled cocktail glasses and garnish with the basil paste. Transfer the rosewater to an atomiser and spray over the sorbet. Serve immediately, garnished with a basil leaf each.

Spain is a country of wines, and Spanish wines are generally quite high in alcohol: almost all have 12% alcohol or more. Barcelona is surrounded by the vineyards of Empordá, Girona and Maresme in the north and north-west and the lush region of the Penedès in the south-west.

Spain, and Catalonia in particular, are home not only to amazing wines and some very enjoyable beers, but also to the (in)famous sangría, which is – how should one put it – very popular around Mallorcan resorts.

In Barcelona, the bars on Las Ramblas serve sangría that is so sweet it almost sticks to the palate, but properly prepared it can be truly delightful. It also has a refreshing, sparkling sibling, the *sangría de cava*, which comes from the Penedès region around Barcelona. In summer, *tinto de verano*, red wine with sparkling, sweetened mineral water, is yet another popular drink in the city's bars.

Barcelona has its very own beer, the 'Moritz', named after the local brewery's Alsatian founder. The brewery runs its own pub in the city centre, which has been refurbished and reopened and now serves refreshing beer on tap.

Spaniards love to have an after-dinner *café*, that is, a short black. Or you could have a *cortado*, which is a short black with a dash of milk, or a *carajillo*, a short black with liqueur or some kind or spirit. Any coffee is usually served together with a glass of ice cubes, especially in summer. Once the coffee has been sweetened to taste, it is poured over the ice cubes to chill and then enjoyed immediately. Other popular drinks to have after dinner are digestifs, most commonly brandy or rum, ice-cold *orujo*, a type of grape marc spirit, or *hierba*, a herb liqueur.

DRINKS

SANGRÍA

SANGRÍA | SANGRIA

If a sangría *is prepared with the right ingredients, it can be enjoyed without any fear of suffering a hangover the next day. There are literally hundreds of methods for preparing* sangría *– some of them quick, some of them slow. However, a really good* sangría *does take a little time, and this particular one is certainly a few leagues above those served in Mallorcan resorts or on Las Ramblas.*

Makes 2 litres (70 fl oz) | **Preparation:** 10 minutes | **Cooking time:** 10 minutes | **Chilling time:** 2 hours

2 tablespoons sugar
1 small cinnamon stick
1 pinch freshly ground
  nutmeg
1 glass cognac or rum
1 bottle dry, young red wine,
  well chilled
Juice of 2 organic oranges
Juice of 1 organic lemon
2 peaches, diced
1 apple, diced
Halved slices of 1 organic
  orange
Lemon- or orange-flavoured
  sparkling mineral water

Heat the sugar in 2 tablespoons water in a saucepan over medium heat, stirring, then add the cinnamon stick. Take the saucepan off the heat as soon as the liquid starts to boil. Leave to cool and add the nutmeg and cognac.

Transfer to a large jug and add the wine and the juices. Add the fruit to the liquid. If you like your *sangría* a bit sweeter, top it up with sweetened sparkling mineral water to taste. Refrigerate the *sangría* for at least 2 hours. Serve with ice cubes.

SANGRÍA DE CAVA

SANGRÍA DE CAVA | CAVA SANGRIA

A different version, sangría de cava, *makes a particularly refreshing summer drink that is just as easily prepared.* Sangría de cava *originated in the immediate surroundings of Barcelona, where sparkling cava wine is produced.*

Makes 1.2 litres (42 fl oz) | **Preparation:** 10 minutes

1 organic orange, quartered
   and sliced
1 organic lemon, sliced
200 ml (7 fl oz) orange
   lemonade
200 ml (7 fl oz) lemonade
400 ml (14 fl oz) Cointreau
400 ml (14 fl oz) dry
   vermouth (Martini
   or Noilly Prat)
Ice cubes to taste
1 bottle cava brut,
   well chilled

Combine the fruit, two types of lemonade, Cointreau and vermouth in a large jug. Add the ice cubes and carefully pour the cava on top, trying to preserve as much of the fizz as possible. Stir gently and serve immediately.

CAVA

If there is a single drink that is inseparably linked with Barcelona, it's cava, the typically Spanish sparkling wine. Cava is a dry sparkling wine that is generally produced from macabeu, parellada and xarel-lo grapes. In Australia, the best-known cava brands are 'Freixenet' and 'Cordoníu', but there are about 100 other vineyards that also make absolutely exquisite cava. One of my personal favourites comes from the 'Agustí Torelló' vineyard.

CREMAT

CREMAT | FLAMBÉ RUM COFFEE

Cremat is particularly popular around the beginning of summer, when people love sitting outside on the beaches until late. Cremat is always prepared fresh. It's also a popular drink served from stalls at community fairs. Cremat is a bit like a mulled wine flambé. It is generally prepared after sunset, and the flambéing process is a little celebration of its own.

Serves 4–6 | **Preparation:** 10 minutes | **Cooking time:** 25 minutes

500 ml (17 fl oz) cachaça (spirit distilled from sugar cane)
500 ml (17 fl oz) brown rum
Zest of ½ an organic lemon, peeled off in a single strip
2 cinnamon sticks
5 coffee beans
5 tablespoons sugar
250 ml (9 fl oz) black coffee

Add the cachaça, rum, lemon zest, cinnamon sticks and coffee beans to a large saucepan. Stir in the sugar until dissolved and heat the mixture over medium heat.

Remove a small amount of the liquid with a ladle. Light the liquid in the ladle and carefully return the burning alcohol to the saucepan to allow the flames to spread across the whole surface.

Leave to burn for a little while, while you prepare the coffee. Keep stirring to ensure that the alcohol burns down slowly. Once the flames get weaker after 15–20 minutes, stir in the coffee and serve in coffee cups.

MOJITO SIN ALCOHOL

MOJITO SIN ALCOHOL | VIRGIN MOJITO

What would a day on Barcelona's beaches be without ending it over a decent cocktail or two? However, sometimes life throws a spanner in the works in the form of random breath testing stations on your way home. Not to worry, though – people in Barcelona are very ingenious, and some beach bars serve delectable virgin mojitos that are almost indistinguishable from their not-so-virtuous cousins. Ginger is added for extra spice and to impart a flavour similar to alcohol. If you still get pulled over by the police, maybe it's the mojitos from the previous night that are still lingering...

Serves 4–6 | **Preparation:** 10 minutes | **Chilling time:** 30 minutes

6–8 organic limes
Fine brown sugar
  to taste
1 medium-sized piece
  of fresh ginger,
  thinly sliced
1 handful of mint
  leaves, torn
Ice cubes
750 ml (26 fl oz) chilled
  mineral water

Slice 1 lime and set aside. Cut the remaining limes into 8 wedges each. Add the brown sugar and pound in a mortar and pestle to squeeze out the juice. Transfer the ginger into a glass carafe and add the sugar and lime juice mixture. Chill for 30 minutes.

Remove the carafe from the refrigerator and add the mint leaves, slices of lime and ice cubes. Top with the mineral water, stir and serve.

Where, if not here? In Barcelona, there's always time and a relaxing place for a coffee.

Olive oil is an absolute must in Barcelonian cuisine, as in all Spanish cooking. When I say olive oil, I always mean cold-pressed oil of the highest quality. My favourite is the oil pressed from the tiny arbequina olives, which are very typically Catalan, although they were only introduced to Catalonia from the Middle East in the 17th century. Arbequinas produce a richly aromatic and fruity oil. For me, the best olive oils come from the region around Lleida and the counties of Siurana near Tarragona and Garrotxa north of Barcelona. For basic frying and deep-frying, it's perfectly fine to use sunflower oil or peanut oil, though.

Barcelonian cuisine works with a number of very special ingredients. A typical example would be a *picada*, which forms an essential part of many different recipes and is used to thicken liquids and to enhance the natural flavour and aroma of foods. A *picada* usually consists of dry bread, hazelnuts, almonds, flat-leaf (Italian) parsley and garlic, but there are endless variations of this basic recipe. Catalan cooking also relies extensively on *ñora* or *nyora* peppers. These plum-sized, round, reddish-black dried peppers have a mildly spicy flavour and appear again and again in Catalan recipes, including in a local take on paella. They also form an essential part of *romesco* sauce (see page 261) and all of its variations. As these peppers impart a lovely golden-red hue to foods, they are also used as a substitute for saffron. Sourcing *nyora* peppers may be a bit of a challenge – alternatively use other mildly spicy peppers or chillies or mildly spicy chilli powder for heat and flavour or saffron for colour.

Classics of Spanish and Catalan cooking such as *all i oli* and *samfaina* are, of course, a must in a lot of the recipes in this book. However, their use is by no means limited to this regional cuisine, and they complement an endless number of dishes.

BASICS

SALSA MAHONESA

SALSA MAHONESA | MAYONNAISE

*Any Catalan cook worth their salt would,
of course, never use mayonnaise from a jar,
only home-made. While the French may claim
that they invented mayonnaise, Spaniards are
adamant that this sauce originated in Mahón,
the capital of Menorca. Quite possibly they're
both right. Always use very fresh
eggs of the highest quality.*

Makes 1 small jar | **Preparation:** 15 minutes

2 fresh egg yolks
1 teaspoon lemon juice or vinegar
300 ml (10½ fl oz) olive oil
1 pinch salt

Beat the egg yolks in a bowl with a hand
whisk. Add a little lemon juice and continue
whisking. Add the olive oil, first drop by
drop, then in a thin stream. Continue to whisk
until the mayonnaise is well combined, with
a creamy consistency. Season with salt and
more lemon juice (or vinegar).

Mayonnaise made from fresh eggs must
be consumed immediately.

ALL I OLI

ALL I OLI | AÏOLI

*This cold garlic sauce is commonly referred to
as 'garlic mayonnaise'. However, in contrast to
mayonnaise, it contains no egg, only garlic (all)
and olive oil (oli) as well as some salt. The recipe
is as easy as it is delicious. All i oli matches
perfectly with any type of fideo pasta dishes,
rice dishes, fish or grilled meats, but it is just
as enjoyable on plain, fresh bread.*

Makes 1 small jar | **Preparation:** 15 minutes

1 garlic clove, coarsely chopped
½ teaspoon salt
125–250 ml (4–9 fl oz) olive oil
Lemon juice for seasoning

THE CLASSIC
Pound the garlic and salt to a paste in a
mortar and pestle.

Gradually stir in the olive oil, first drop
by drop, then in a thin stream, until you
have a thick cream. *All i oli* has the perfect
consistency if you can turn the mortar
upside down with the sauce clinging to
the bottom without dripping. Season with
a little lemon juice.

IF YOU'RE IN A RUSH
For a quicker version, combine the same
ingredients plus 1 egg yolk with a stick
blender for 1 minute and season with a
little lemon juice. This sauce is a little
milder than 'genuine' *all i oli.*

ROMESCO

SALSA ROMESCO | ROMESCO SAUCE

Romesco sauce originally comes from the region around Tarragona, but these days it has become a staple of Catalan cuisine. Romesco is most commonly served with grilled vegetables and fish.

Makes 1 jar | **Preparation:** 20 minutes
Soaking time: 2 hours | **Marinating time:** 12 hours

1 nyora pepper or 1 small red, dried chilli and/or
chilli powder to taste; see also the tip on page 166
10 blanched almonds
10 blanched hazelnuts
½ stale bread roll
A little vinegar water for soaking the bread roll
1½ tablespoons tomato paste (concentrated purée)
1 garlic clove, crushed
Olive oil

Remove the stem base and core from the nyora pepper and soak the pepper in hot water for about 2 hours. Use it whole or scrape the flesh off the skin.

Toast the almonds and hazelnuts in a pan over high heat. Soak the bread roll in vinegar water.

Grind the almonds and hazelnuts to a medium-fine grind. Squeeze out excess water from the bread roll and tear into small pieces. Add to the ground nuts together with the pepper flesh, tomato paste, salt and garlic. Stir in a generous amount of olive oil to make a thick sauce. Season again and set aside to rest and allow the flavours to marry. Ideally leave the sauce to stand overnight.

Covered with a layer of olive oil, this sauce will keep for 3–4 weeks in the refrigerator. Bring to room temperature and stir before serving.

FUMET

FUMET | FISH STOCK

An aromatic fish or seafood stock is essential for flavouring many soup, rice and pasta dishes.

Makes 1 litre (35 fl oz) | **Preparation:** 25 minutes
Cooking time: 30 minutes

1 kg (2 lb 4 oz) white fish, plus fish carcasses,
heads, skin and bones
Olive oil for frying
1 garlic clove, unpeeled
1 carrot, diced
1 small leek, thickly sliced
1 onion, coarsely diced
1 green capsicum (pepper), coarsely diced
1 ripe tomato, coarsely diced
4–5 sprigs flat-leaf (Italian) parsley, chopped

Wash the fish and fish carcasses under running water. Chop any larger pieces.

Heat a large saucepan over high heat, add the olive oil and garlic and sear briefly. Add all of the vegetables and the parsley and continue to fry, stirring. Add the fish and keep stirring until it starts to fall apart. Deglaze the pan with 1 litre (35 fl oz) hot water, season with salt and boil for 20–30 minutes, skimming off any scum. Strain the soup through a sieve, squeezing all of the juices out of the fish carcasses and vegetables. The stock is now ready to use.

You can also prepare this stock from fish and seafood; simply use the heads and carcasses of lobster, crayfish, crabs etc. and pound them in a mortar and pestle first. Reduce the amount of fish accordingly.

ESCALIVADA

ESCALIVADA | GRILLED VEGETABLES

Escalivada *is a typical Catalan side dish that can be served warm or cold. Stored in jars and covered with a layer of olive oil, it will keep for several weeks in the refrigerator.*

Serves 4 | **Preparation:** 10 minutes
Baking time: 50 minutes
Resting time: 10 minutes
Marinating time: 15 minutes

4 eggplants (aubergines), cut into bite-sized pieces
4 large red capsicums (peppers)
4 onions, coarsely diced
2 garlic cloves
Sea salt flakes
Olive oil for drizzling

Preheat the oven to 160°C (320°F). Place the eggplant pieces, capsicums and diced onions on a baking tray. Bake on the middle rack of the preheated oven until soft, about 40–50 minutes. Turn repeatedly, especially the capsicums. Switch the oven to the grill (broiler) function for the last 10 minutes.

Leave the vegetables in the oven until the capsicum skins have blackened. If the eggplant and onion pieces turn too dark, remove them from the oven. Take the capsicums out of the oven, wrap them in newspaper and set them aside to rest for 10 minutes. Peel the capsicums and remove the stem bases and cores. Cut the vegetables into strips and transfer these to a bowl. Peel and mince the garlic and add to the vegetables. Season with sea salt flakes and freshly ground black pepper, drizzle with olive oil and leave to marinate for about 15 minutes.

PEBROTS VERMELLS AL FORN I ALINIATS

PIMIENTOS ROJOS ASADOS
MARINATED GRILLED CAPSICUMS

Grilled, marinated capsicums are a popular side dish for fish, poultry or grilled meats. They can be easily prepared ahead and stored in the refrigerator for several days.

Serves 4 | **Preparation:** 10 minutes
Resting time: 10 minutes
Cooking and baking time: 55 minutes

4 large red capsicums (peppers)
100 ml (3½ fl oz) fino sherry
1 teaspoon honey
2 tablespoons olive oil

Preheat the oven to high heat using the grill (broiler) function. Arrange the capsicums on a baking tray in a single layer and roast in the oven for 40–50 minutes until blackened all over. Remove from the oven, wrap in newspaper and set aside to rest for 10 minutes. Peel the capsicums and remove the stem bases and cores. Cut into strips about 2.5 cm (1 inch) wide.

Heat the sherry, honey and olive oil in a saucepan with a little salt. Add the capsicum strips and simmer for 3 minutes. Take off the heat and leave to cool. Covered with the broth and stored in screw-top jars, these marinated capsicums will keep for several days in the refrigerator.

SAMFAINA

SAMFAINA | ROAST VEGETABLES

Samfaina, *a Mediterranean recipe for roast vegetables, is a very popular side dish for fish, poultry and meats in classic Catalan cuisine.* Samfaina *has been used in traditional cooking for centuries, and its name is said to be derived from the Latin word* symphonia *(harmony).*

Serves 4 | **Preparation:** 5 minutes
Cooking time: 30 minutes
Marinating time: 3 hours

Olive oil for frying
1 garlic clove, crushed
1 green capsicum (pepper), coarsely diced
2 onions, diced
1 large eggplant (aubergine), coarsely diced
1 zucchini (courgette), coarsely diced
2 peeled tomatoes (from a can)
1–2 teaspoons dried thyme
1 teaspoon sweet paprika

Heat a little olive oil in a frying pan over medium heat and fry the garlic until golden brown.

Add the capsicum and continue to fry for 10 minutes. Add the onions and cook for another 5 minutes. Stir in the remaining vegetables, thyme and paprika. Season to taste and cook until soft, about 5–10 minutes.

Set aside for 2–3 hours before serving to allow the flavours to marry. *Samfaina* tastes best reheated.

TRINXAT

TRINXAT | CABBAGE AND POTATOES

Trinxat, *a dish prepared from cabbage and potatoes, originally comes from the region north of Barcelona. It is usually served as a snack or a side dish.*

Serves 4 | **Preparation:** 10 minutes
Cooking time: 40 minutes

1 white cabbage
2 large potatoes
Olive oil for frying
4 slices bacon
2 garlic cloves, thinly sliced

Remove the outer leaves and hard cores from the cabbage, then cut the cabbage into coarse pieces. Peel the potatoes and cut into pieces about 2.5 cm (1 inch) in size. Boil both in salted water for about 20 minutes in separate pots.

Heat a large, deep pan over medium heat. Add the olive oil and bacon and fry until golden brown. Remove from the pan and set aside. Fry the garlic in the same pan until golden brown. As soon as the garlic starts to colour, add the drained cabbage and potatoes. Lower the heat and warm through, stirring carefully. As soon as you have a uniform mixture, increase the heat again and fry the *trinxat* like you would a tortilla until golden brown on both sides.

Garnish with the bacon and serve. Alternatively, dice the bacon and fold in before frying.

POBLE NOU

BORN/LA RIBERA

1 – La Pitarra
La Pitarra is a long-established restaurant that is very typically Catalan. It has a lovely, cosy interior, and the staff are incredibly helpful. I particularly recommend the game and venison specialties served in autumn.
Carrer d'Avinyó, 56

2 – Agut
The Agut was once mainly frequented by those 'in the know', but became very popular in the boom years right after the 1992 Olympics. These days it is firmly established as one of the reliably good restaurants in the city.
Carrer d'En Gignàs, 16

3 – Cuines Santa Caterina
This restaurant is inside the Mercat de Santa Caterina. Its chefs cook whatever is best on the market on the day. Its name, *cuines* means 'kitchens', as this restaurant serves delicious dishes from a range of different cuisines.
Av. de Francesc Cambó, 16

4 – 7 Portes
The 7 Portes is another traditional restaurant that has been around for almost a century and still reliably serves good, classic Catalan food.
Passeig Isabel II, 14

5 – Peps Buffet
This small restaurant serves a buffet of classic Catalan dishes in an ever-changing variety. Don't go here if you're only after a little bite! The buffet serves first starters and soups, then a range of mains and desserts.
Carrer de Grunyí, 5

6 – Restaurante Petra
This restaurant directly on the walls of the Basilica of Santa Maria del Mar is one of the very few in the area that do not cater exclusively to the tourist market.
Carrer dels Sombrerers, 13

7 – Patisseria Bubó Born
The Bubó, also next to the Basilica of Santa Maria del Mar, serves chocolate and simply exquisite confectioneries that are nothing if not works of art. Its sister shop next door serves breakfast and tapas.
Carrer de les Caputxes, 10

8 – La Vinya del Senyor
This wine bar is one of the traditional addresses in this quarter that has remained relatively unaffected by tourism. Its clientele is always a very pleasant mix of people from all sorts of backgrounds enjoying a huge selection of tapas.
Plaza Santa Maria, 5

9 – El Xampanyet
This is one of the best-known tapas bars in the quarter and always worth a visit. Do not leave without having tried the *xampán*, the sparkling house wine served in a swing-top bottle. Plus there are obviously the tapas, which always attract a crowd.
Carrer de Montcada, 22

10 – Bar Celta Pulpería
This bar serves Galician wines from porcelain bowls together with genuine Galician tapas such as *pulpo a la gallega*, or stewed octopus. It gets very busy in the evenings and on weekends.
Carrer de la Princesa, 50

11 – Nou Celler
This small, friendly restaurant right in the heart of the old town, near the Picasso museum, serves classic Catalan cuisine and tapas. Its owner, Elisabet Roldán, greets her guests herself with her own unique warmth.
Carrer de la Princesa, 16

12 – La Paradeta
The queue outside this restaurant just before it opens says it all. You get to choose your own fresh fish and seafood at its food stalls right behind the CCB, the old market of the Born quarter, and your choice is then prepared immediately. Once your meal is ready, your number is called and you pick up your treasure directly from the kitchen.
Carrer Comercial, 7

BARRI GÒTIC

13 – Caelum
This small café is called 'Caelum, delicias y otras tentaciones de Monasterio' for a reason. All of the delicacies it sells, from confectionery to cheeses, are prepared by nuns or monks.
Carrer de la Palla, 8

14 – Orolíquido
This genuine boutique for premium cooking oils is located right next to Caelum. You can spend a fortune here on oils, in keeping with the quality of offer, but for your money you'll definitely get the very finest olive oils in all of Spain and its neighbouring countries.
Carrer de la Palla, 8

15 – Ocaña
The Ocaña, named after an artist-activist of the 1970s, was reopened three years ago after it had been closed for several years for extensive refurbishment. It was an immediate success and is now one of Barcelona's most beautiful cafés/bars as far as I'm concerned.
Plaça Reial, 13–15

16 – Els 4 Gats
The Els 4 Gats is a classic Barcelona restaurant and café that was made famous in the 20th century when Picasso often met his friends here while he lived in the city.
Carrer de Montsió, 3

EL RAVAL

17 – Fonda España
This restaurant is located in the old, refurbished Hotel España and has two spectacularly beautiful old dining halls. Its dishes are expertly prepared by the master cook Berasategui.
Carrer de Sant Pau, 9–11

18 – El Cafetí
The Cafetí is another of the traditional Art Nouveau restaurants, perhaps a touch indulgent with its velvet, but very pleasant nonetheless.If you find *suprema de bacalau* on the menu when visiting, that is, bacalao with leeks and apples, do not leave without trying it!
Carrer de Sant Rafael, 18

19 – El Quim De La Boquería
The Boquería markets are not only a shopping experience, but also offer excellent dining. The Quim serves small plates of delicious food at inexpensive prices. The only problem is that getting – or keeping – a seat is almost like playing musical chairs: if you're too slow (or not determined enough), you stand no chance.
Les Rambles, 91

20 – Pinotxo Bar
This bar is on the right side of the Boqueria markets. Expect the same seating challenges as in the Quim (see opposite)!
Les Rambles, 91

21– Quimet & Quimet
Only a few years ago, the Quimet & Quimet was THE insider address as far as tapas bars were concerned. Today, it is widely known, much loved and very popular, but it is worth making the effort. This bar is so successful that it can afford to have opening hours that are rather unusual for Barcelona.
Carrer del Poeta Cabanyes, 25

SANT ANTONI
22 – Fàbrica Moritz
The Fàbrica Moritz has fresh beer on tap straight out of the cellar. Its refreshing beer is served in a setting that is very unusual for Barcelona. A proper restaurant was opened in 2016 in addition to the existing beer bar.
Ronda de Sant Antoni, 39–41

EIXAMPLE
23 – El Nacional
The El Nacional was opened in early 2015. It is very much reminiscent of a Belle Époque market hall and houses five different restaurants under a single roof. Its grill section serves Barcelona's most expensive beef (sourced from Nebraska or Kobe).
Passeig de Gràcia, 24

24 – Cinc Sentits
The Cinc Sentits ('five senses') truly lives up to its name, serving first-rate Catalan cuisine. Its food is pricey, but it's worth every cent.
Carrer d'Aribau, 58

25 – Osmosis
Osmosis has been one of my favourite restaurants for years. Once a week, chef Frederic Fernandez creates a 7-course menu, which is all he'll serve that night. The only choice guests have is whether they want three, five or seven courses. The dishes are always surprisingly innovative, imaginative and incredibly delicious. By focusing exclusively on these seven courses, the kitchen makes sure they work only with the freshest of ingredients. I suggest that you leave the choice of wines to the sommelier,

Ingasi Montes. Some of the recipes in this book are from Osmosis.
Carrer d'Aribau, 100

26 – Restaurante Tragaluz
The Tragaluz is a traditional restaurant that consistently lives up to its excellent reputation and has done so with ease for many years. It serves fine, modern Catalan cuisine at prices that are entirely reasonable for what it has on offer.
Passatge de la Concepció, 5

27 – La Semproniana
The Semproniana has a very unconventional interior, as it is housed in a former printing shop. With very good food at reasonable prices, this was my favourite restaurant for a long time.
Carrer del Rosselló, 148

28 – La Polpa
This restaurant forms part of a chain (Flamant, Balthazar, Les Quinze Nits, Market in Barcelona) and always has excellent food at reasonable prices. Its lunchtime menu is particularly good and inexpensive.
Carrer d'Enric Granados, 69

29 – La Palmera
If there are two of you, I highly recommend you try the degustation menu with three starters and three mains per person.
Carrer d'Enric Granados, 57

30 – Etapes
The Etapes opened right in the middle of an economic crisis, but its team has been successful by serving good food at reasonable prices, and it has been going well without compromising on quality.
Carrer d'Enric Granados, 10

31 – Cacao Sampaka
Carrer del Consell de Cent, 292

32 – La Vinoteca Torres
Torres, a global player in the world of wines, opened its showcase Vinoteca at an expensive location a few years ago, but it is definitely worth stopping there.
Passeig de Gràcia, 78

33 – Gadgets Cuina
The Gadgets stocks just about everything a hobby chef's heart

desires. Find anything here that you might want or need for putting the perfect finishing touches on your cooking.
Carrer d'Aragó, 249

POBLE NOU
34 – Dos Cielos
This restaurant in the Hotel Meliá Barcelona Sky is one of Barcelona's best addresses. Run by the Torres brothers, its chefs continuously surprise guests with a huge range of delicious dishes ranging from homely to elegant.
Carrer de Pere IV, 272–286

35 – ESHOB, Escola Superior d'Hostaleria de Barcelona
If you dine in the School of Hotel Management, you'll be served food cooked by future chefs and waited on by future maître d's. The prices are very reasonable and well worth taking the minute risk that something might be less than perfect.
Passeig del Taulat, 243

GRÀCIA, SARRIÀ, ST GERVASI
36 – Bar Tomás
Come here to enjoy the only genuine 'patatas bravas' in Barcelona!
Carrer Major de Sarrià, 49

37 – Oli Sal
A small specialist supplier of fine cooking salts and oils. This is where the city's best chefs shop.
Travessera de Gràcia 149

BARCELONETA
38 – Cal Pinxo
This seafood restaurant in Barceloneta has been serving consistently high-quality fish and seafood for decades.
Plaça de Pau Vila, 1

CANYELLES
Cal Manelet
If you ever get to spend some time in the resort towns of Sitges or Villanova south-west of Barcelona, try to visit this true gem of traditional Catalan cooking. It is located in the village of Canyelles, about 12 km inland, right below the castle. Some of the photos in this book were taken there.
Crta. Vilafranca a Vilanova, 5

INDEX

THANKS

Our warmest thanks go to the following restaurants: Bar Celta Pulperia, Cal Manelet, Cal Pinxo, Bar Tomás, Caelum, Nou Celler, El Xampanyet, El Cafetí, La Paradeta, Osmosis. And to my friend Marc Robles i Montes. All have made a huge contribution to this book.

Published in 2024 by Murdoch Books, an imprint of Allen & Unwin
First published in 2017 by Christian Verlag GmbH, Munich

Murdoch Books Australia
Cammeraygal Country
83 Alexander Street
Crows Nest NSW 2065
Phone: +61 (0)2 8425 0100
murdochbooks.com.au
info@murdochbooks.com.au

Murdoch Books UK
Ormond House
26–27 Boswell Street
London WC1N 3JZ
Phone: +44 (0) 20 8785 5995
murdochbooks.co.uk
info@murdochbooks.co.uk

For corporate orders and custom publishing, contact our business development team at salesenquiries@murdochbooks.com.au

ENGLISH-LANGUAGE PUBLISHER: Jane Morrow

AUTHOR: Stephan Mitsch

PHOTOGRAPHER: Arnold Pöschl

TRANSLATOR: Claudia Koch-McQuillan

PRODUCTION DIRECTOR: Lou Playfair

Murdoch Books acknowledges the Traditional Owners of the Country on which we live and work. We pay our respects to all Aboriginal and Torres Strait Islander Elders, past and present.

ISBN 978 1 76150 043 5

 A catalogue record for this book is available from the National Library of Australia

A catalogue record for this book is available from the British Library

Colour reproduction by Splitting Image Colour Studio Pty Ltd, Wantirna, Victoria
Printed by 1010 Printing International Limited, China

OVEN GUIDE: You may find cooking times vary depending on the oven you are using. For fan-forced ovens, as a general rule, set the oven temperature to 20°C (35°F) lower than indicated in the recipe.

IMPORTANT: Those who might be at risk from the effects of salmonella poisoning (the elderly, pregnant women, young children and those suffering from immune deficiency diseases) should consult their doctor with any concerns about eating raw eggs. Please ensure that all seafood and beef to be eaten raw or lightly cooked are very fresh and of the highest quality.

10 9 8 7 6 5 4 3 2 1

12/24